21 Weeks to True Prosperity

Biblical Principles for
Wellness and (True) Wealth

by
Craig Carey Brenton

Contents

INTRODUCTION

What is the source of our wealth? Most Christians would answer that question with "God Almighty." Many Christians, however, would credit themselves for their success with perhaps a little help from the Lord. Still, others would say they simply pulled themselves up by their own bootstraps with zero help from God or anyone else. Many non-Christians will tell you their success has been due primarily to their work ethic. The humbler non-Christians may attribute their success to their parents, their friends, or just good luck.

However, I seldom hear successful individuals credit the "prosperity gospel" for their success. Surprisingly, however, you can turn your television on any time and hear some word of faith preachers advocate what is often described as a "name it and claim it" ticket to wealth. If I need a new refrigerator, according to this gospel, I can simply claim it in the name of Jesus and expect God to provide it.

No, you will not find the "Name it and claim it" prosperity gospel of the word of faith preachers here.

Yet, if you decide to adopt the twenty-one biblical precepts outlined in this book, your diligence in this pursuit of excellence will easily place you in the top 1 percent of your company, business, or school. No, I'm not guaranteeing you a 4.0 grade point average in school or your rise to CEO of your company. However, I do guarantee that you will be multiplying your opportunities for and probability of success above 99 percent of your coworkers' or fellow students'.

This book will examine and advocate a real prosperity gospel anchored upon the tenets of the Bible, both Old and New Testament.

Twenty-one specific principles drawn from Scripture constitute the basis for the pursuit of true biblical prosperity. However, you will not get rich by visualizing yourself as a billionaire, repeating a particular Bible verse, or claiming a Hollywood mansion for yourself in the name of the Lord.

In this book, I will be your life coach. "Yet," you ask, "why do I even need coaching in this time of unlimited educational opportunity?" The answer: In America today, social media, the internet, television, and schools all militate against your adopting the spiritual philosophy of excellence advocated by the Bible. Why has the Bible consistently been the best-selling book in the world? Unlike any other self-help book, the Bible contains the real seeds for your success in business, money, relationships, and, ultimately, your eternity with Christ. If you are pursuing the secular expectations of our culture to be accepted, you may be confused, weak, and unable to achieve stability and growth in your relationships, your career, and your spiritual life. You may live paycheck to paycheck with broken relationships, failed marriages, and emotional turmoil, resulting in an unstable, unhappy, and unhealthy existence.

By embracing the twenty-one principles outlined here, you are establishing a foundation for the pursuit of excellence in your workplace, your business, your family, and your relationship with God. Even if you are not a Christian and you are not interested in becoming a believer, by adhering to these principles, you will still put yourself in position for success in every arena of life except, of course, your relationship with God.

Real Prosperity equals the pursuit of excellence and success in business, family, career, and your relationship with God.

This is the only book you will find anywhere that incorporates the 21 most important biblical values as a prescription for living a life of excellence and shows you exactly how to develop the discipline to achieve that real prosperity. The book is unique also in that we teach the biblical methodology for healing and how real prosperity can only be achieved if we are willing to fight to defend our religious, economic, and political freedoms. There is no prosperity in tyranny.

Why do I care about your real prosperity? I love my God, my family, and my country. If America is to survive and thrive, Americans need to reawaken their faith, their dependence upon God, and his word. The principles that I propound in this book will ensure that the people who read it will be prepared for leadership in business, government, and their families.

I personally have been married to the same wonderful and beautiful woman since 1980. My wife, Cindy, and I have raised six children, five of whom are adopted. They range in age from forty to our youngest son, Elliott, age fifteen, still at home. Truly, they challenged Cindy and me as parents throughout their upbringing. I have chased down bank robbers for the FBI, litigated jury trials as an attorney, and successfully managed my own investment securities practice. I also served as Executive Assistant Superintendent of the Oregon State Police for several years and state treasurer of a major political party.

For over four years, I served as the business news analyst and reporter for a daily morning news and lifestyle program in Portland, Oregon.

I am not telling you this to brag about my accomplishments. You, too, can and must also arrive at your own "Paul on the road to Damascus" moment. Why not arrive there now? The following chapters will instruct, coach, and encourage you in building your own future upon a biblical foundation. Jesus speaks about this foundation in Luke 6:48: "He is like a man which built an house, and digged deep, and laid the foundation on a rock: and when the

3

flood arose, the stream beat vehemently upon that house, and could not shake it: for it was founded upon a rock."

Finally, if you are reading this book solely because it piques your intellectual curiosity, you are wasting your time. This book is a tool for creating a lifestyle for victorious living and success—nothing less.

I encourage you to take notes as you read and practice the concepts outlined in each chapter. Each week, memorize the principle you are studying. For example, commit to memory "Be generous" when you encounter that principle in week #11. Then, the next time you have an opportunity to help someone, the need for generosity will immediately be uppermost in your mind.

Never allow yourself to feel defeated or depressed or to give up when you fail to implement a principle you have already studied and practiced. Although we will eventually reach proficiency with each principle, we will never attain perfection in this life. However, be encouraged each time you find yourself exercising a principle you have learned. For example, a few weeks ago, I was on a roll displaying courage and optimism in major financial and investment decisions. Yet, on Friday morning, I learned that one of my investments had deteriorated badly. Suddenly, I was distraught and unhappy for about an hour. Finally, I realized how I had allowed my fear and worry over that outcome to depress me and transform me into a bear for my wife, Cindy, and my son, Elliott, to live with. Becoming self-aware and making the conscious decision to practice courage and optimism, I turned from my pity party and recalled that I knew how to be courageous. I started looking forward to the probability that my investment misfortune was only temporary. Markets go both down and back up again! I reminded myself that even if this investment continued to do poorly, my physical and financial health would still be fine. I focused on the financial, health, and family blessings God has afforded me over the years. Suddenly, my fearful attitude was quashed. I moved on with a positive attitude for the rest of the day.

Chapter 1
Where Did the "Name It and Claim It" Prosperity Gospel Come From?

The Prosperity Gospel is believed to have originated in the late 19th century in America. The prosperity gospel evolved from the rugged individualism of the 19th century and frontier America. By the sheer power of your will, you can command the Holy Spirit to give you what you want if you just have faith. According to the prosperity gospel, we use God to get what we want. Of course, according to traditional Christian teaching, God uses us to accomplish what he wants for our lives.

Televangelist Kenneth Hagin is usually credited as a founder of the modern-day prosperity gospel in the mid-1970's. Other televangelists have expanded on Hugin's theme.

To boil down this theology today, it is simply the more you give, the more you get. The biblical support for this belief is found in 2 Corinthians 9:6-8, "Remember this: Whoever sows sparingly will also reap sparingly, and whoever sows generously will also reap generously."

What do you get? Money! Financial wealth and physical health. Some Word of Faith preachers would also add "power" to that equation. Of course, generally, the preacher advocating this theology suggests that the "giving" should be to his ministry. I don't generally hear a "name it and claim it "pastor urging you to give to the Billy Graham Evangelistic Association, Samaritan's Purse, or Goodwill. The televangelist's congregation buys into the idea of "giving in order to get..." This may be a retired secretary who is living on a sparse Social Security check. She drains her bank account in order to send the prosperity minister her money in anticipation of winning the lottery or receiving an unexpected inheritance. Often, the televangelist will show video testimony of a couple who were shocked when they were blessed with a windfall of money just after donating a substantial sum to his ministry. The exploitation of his loyal viewer's greed or desperation is obvious. Consequently, many of these pastors become exceedingly wealthy.

The prosperity gospel is often referred to as the Word of Faith movement. Some Word of Faith pastors even teach that wealth is a sign of God's favor and blessing. Poverty signifies your lack of faith or may even reflect your sinfulness.

David W. Jones outlines five errors of prosperity gospel teaching in his book, "Health, Wealth, and Happiness: Has the Prosperity Gospel Overshadowed the Gospel of Christ?" (Kregel, 2010):

1. The Abrahamic covenant is a means to material entitlement.

2. Jesus's atonement extends to the "sin" of material poverty.

3. Christians give in order to gain material compensation from God.

4. Faith is a self-generated spiritual force that leads to prosperity.

5. Prayer is a tool to force God to grant prosperity

Of course, the Bible does not teach that it is a sin to be poor. Jesus was poor, and his disciples had surrendered any desire for worldly riches to be with him. Indeed, at one point, Jesus says, "Foxes have holes and birds of the air have nests, but the Son of Man has no place to lay his head." (Matthew 18:20, NIV).

The Bible never says that giving to God is a quid pro quo arrangement. According to Deuteronomy 14:23, (TLB), "The purpose of tithing (giving) is to teach you to put God first in your life."

Faith is not self-made or self-generated. According to the scripture, "For it is by grace you have been saved, through faith— and this [is] not from yourselves, it is the gift of God— 2:9 [this is] not by works, so that no one can boast." Ephesians 2:8.

God is not a genie in a bottle. We cannot summon him through prayer to follow our orders. Yet, many word of faith preachers claim that we can simply command healing, wealth and sometimes power simply by issuing a directive to God in prayer.

Chapter 2
Who Does Not Want to Be Rich?

In 1965, when I was eleven years old and growing up in Baltimore, my dad lost his steady job as a bus driver with the Baltimore Transit Company. Dad had returned from fighting in Europe with the US Army in World War II. He had supported my mom, my two older brothers, and me in his working-class job. However, after losing this job at age forty-five, he was never able to hold down a steady, good-paying job again. Our family struggled just to pay the bills on my mom's paycheck as a secretary working for the Baltimore public schools. Unfortunately, just a few years later, in 1972, my parents split up permanently. Twelve years earlier, in 1960, my dad had joined a radio church in Pasadena, California, which was led by Herbert W. Armstrong. Mr. Armstrong taught and believed in what today is better known as prosperity gospel, upon which he based his "seven laws of success" (Gerald Flurry, Philadelphia Church of God, January 2017). My dad embraced his new religion with amazing alacrity. After his shift driving the bus ended each day, he sat by his radio to hear the latest sermon from Herbert Armstrong, a former advertising executive turned radio preacher. After listening to Mr. Armstrong for about a year, his new church started sending my dad its flagship magazine, "The Plain Truth."

As a little kid, I would thumb through the pages of The Plain Truth and other mailings my dad received from this church. I would see photos of lavish homes with swimming pools accompanying acres of manicured lawns. This apparently represented what Mr. Armstrong was doing with the money Dad was sending him from his bus driver's paycheck. Over the next four years, my dad went from sending Mr. Armstrong 10 percent of his paycheck to almost all of it. Obviously, Dad was hopeful of some time in the future receiving the same good fortune Mr. Armstrong had, either in this life or the next.

Meanwhile, my mom struggled to pay the mortgage on the small, spartan home we lived in. At one point, my aunt brought boxes of groceries to our family. My mom's income as a secretary simply didn't cover the bills and provide for the appetites of her three sons.

Soon after, Mom and Dad's relationship devolved into screaming matches, with my mom pleading for my dad to stop sending his paycheck to Mr. Armstrong and my dad shouting that God demanded that he do so.

In November 1964, my dad finally moved out of our home and rented his own apartment. Soon after, he started failing to show up for work. In January 1965, he was fired. However, Mr. Armstrong, by contrast, was reeling in millions of dollars in tithes and offerings from his loyal radio ministry followers. The New York Times reported that by 1978, the Radio Church of God was taking in $70 million per year ("Church on Coast Is Placed in Receivership," special to the New York Times, January 5, 1979). It is most unfortunate when poor, wannabe-rich people are taken advantage of by wealthy church leaders seeking their own fortunes at the expense of their flock. It is even more tragic when those leaders, often in the public forum on TV and radio, cause nonbelievers to view the true Christian churches as frauds.

President Abraham Lincoln once said, "God must sure love the common people. He sure made a lot of them." Note Lincoln didn't say "God must sure love rich people. He sure made a lot of them."

Of course, he could have said, "God loves common people who want to get rich. He sure made a lot of them." That would certainly be accurate today. The church of the modern-day prosperity gospel is the church of the wannabe-rich man and woman. That's why "Word of Faith" churches are flourishing today, with massive congregations on television and radio and in huge sanctuaries across America. These pastors are also unapologetically beseeching their congregations to give them large sums of money. One pastor recently bragged that he had several private jets. Of course, the jets were paid for by his followers with their hard-earned money in the form of donations to his ministry and the purchase of his books. Word of Faith pastors often live in gated mansions on large estates built on the income from their television and radio congregants.

Word of Faith pastors often teaches that the Bible can guarantee your prosperity as long as you tithe and present your offerings to the church. Much of the prosperity gospel is also based upon this Bible verse: "Bring ye all the tithes into the storehouse, that there may be meat in mine house, and prove me now herewith, saith the Lord of hosts, if I will not open you the windows of heaven, and pour you out a blessing, that there shall not be room enough to receive it" (Malachi 3, 8-). We find more support in Philippians 4:19 (KJV): "My God shall supply all your need according to his riches in glory by Christ Jesus." 3 John 1:2 (KJV): "Beloved, I wish above all things that thou mayest prosper and be in health, even as thy soul prospereth." If God will pour out a blessing so big you have trouble receiving it, obviously, you are incented to give to the church. The implication is that the more you give, the more you get! Certainly, if we google the net worth of these preachers, the prosperity gospel is working for them. However, God's will is certainly not for everyone to get rich. According to Luke 6:35, "Love your enemies. Do good to them. And don't be concerned that they won't repay you." Just prior to that, we find in Luke 6:34, "And if you lend money to those who can repay you, what good is that? Even the most wicked will lend to their own kind for full return."

Again, in Luke 12:16-21, Jesus uses a parable to admonish the rich person who stores up money, real estate, stocks, bank accounts, or any other worldly goods instead of pursuing the kingdom of God:

The ground of a certain rich man yielded an abundant harvest. He thought to himself, "What shall I do? I have no place to store my crops." Then he said, "This is what I'll do. I will tear down my barns and build bigger ones, and there, I will store my surplus grain. And I'll say to myself, "You have plenty of grain laid up for many years. Take life easy; eat, drink and be merry." But God said to him, "You fool! This very night your life will be demanded from you. Then who will get what you have prepared for yourself?" This is how it will be with whoever stores up things for themselves but is not rich toward God.

In his Bibliotheca Sacra article "A Theological Evaluation of the Prosperity Gospel," theologian Ken Sarles observes how the prosperity gospel claims that "both physical healing and financial prosperity have been provided for in the atonement." (1986). There certainly is biblical support for physical healing. This is evidenced by Christ's many healings and the raising of Lazarus from the dead. We will explore how biblical healing is part of the gospel in chapter 24 and why that is part of the true prosperity we should be pursuing every day of our lives. However, the idea that Jesus will give you a barrel of money if you ask for it is fallacious.

Jesus cautions us about making wealth our goal when he says, "Command those who are rich in this present world not to be arrogant nor to put their hope in wealth, which is so uncertain, but to put their hope in God, who richly provides us with everything for our enjoyment" (1 Timothy 6:17–18). In fact, a rich young ruler spoke to Jesus and asked him what he must do to enter heaven. Jesus replied, "If you want to be perfect, go, sell what you have and give to the poor, and you will have treasure in heaven; and come, follow

Me." (Matthew 19:21). It's instructive that Jesus didn't tell the young ruler to set a goal of becoming a multimillionaire and believe that God would make it happen for him. In fact, the man already had great wealth, and Jesus was telling him to give it all away! Just a little further, in Matthew 19:24, Jesus says, "It is easier for a camel to pass through the eye of a needle, than for a rich man to enter into the kingdom of heaven." Certainly, this is not an endorsement of the prosperity gospel or any idea that one of Jesus's primary objectives for Christians is worldly riches. Jesus is really warning us that if our primary objective is wealth, our souls may be headed to hell.

In 1 Timothy, Paul purposely teaches young Timothy that personal wealth should not be our goal (1 Timothy 6:6–8). Paul says, "But those who desire to be rich fall into temptation, into a snare, into many senseless and harmful desires that plunge people into ruin and destruction. For the love of money is the root of all kinds of evil. It is through this craving that some have wandered away from the faith and pierced themselves with many pangs" (1 Timothy 6:9–10). If Paul is saying that a Christian who desires to be rich falls into temptations, then how can a pastor tell his congregation that God wants them to make material wealth their objective? Obviously, God does not want us to fall into temptation and sin.

Finally, Jesus tells us, in Mark 8:36–37, "For what shall it profit a man, if he shall gain the whole world, and lose his own soul? Or what shall a man give in exchange for his soul?" We can easily replace "gain the whole world" with "gain great wealth" and see that God's priority is the saving of our eternal soul, not money.

So, then, are we to conclude that God wants us to be poor, homeless, and living on food stamps or a welfare check?

Absolutely not.

The Puritan work ethic asserts that hard work, honesty, diligence, discipline, and frugality are a result of our adherence to the values delineated in the Holy Bible for Christian living. Further, Scripture teaches us that financial, business, and personal success are the by-products of righteous living. Biblical teaching also admonishes us not to live by the opposite values of dishonesty, sloth, cowardice, extravagance, and boastfulness. Indeed, Jesus warns us that the results of that lifestyle are poverty and death. However, never does the Bible guarantee us a pile of money, health, and worldly success even if we live according to Godly precepts. Indeed, Job was a righteous man who was tormented by sickness, poverty, and the death of his loved ones (book of Job, NKJ). Even Joseph, who appears as a righteous man, suffered from being sold into slavery, wrongly accused of rape, and imprisoned (Genesis 37–40, NKJ). (Even though no sin was attributed to Joseph in the Bible, he too was a sinner needing salvation.)

Jesus summed it up best when responding to Pontius Pilate: "My kingdom is not of this world. If it were, my servants would fight to prevent my arrest by the Jewish leaders. But now my kingdom is from another place" (John 18:36 NIV). So, Jesus's kingdom is not of this world, and we, as Christians, are part of that kingdom. Certainly, then, our prime focus should not be upon maximizing our accumulation of the things of this world.

As a result, we know that God, in his scriptures, has outlined a way for us to live as Christians to achieve true prosperity. However, the aim of that righteous living is not to enrich ourselves on Earth. In fact, the aim is not even to enable us to enter the kingdom of God and spend eternity with Christ, for righteous living itself should be a by-product of our faith in Christ, his death on the cross, and his resurrection three days later. Only faith in Christ's forgiveness of our sins will enable us to share eternity with him.

If you have accepted Christ as your personal Lord and Savior, you are growing in your faith as a Christian. Consequently, we should see the fruit of our faith in a lifestyle that reflects the values described in the Bible for Holy living. If you have not accepted Jesus's forgiveness of your sins as a result of his death on the cross and resurrection, you still may greatly benefit by embracing the values and lifestyle described in the Bible and enumerated with clarity in the following chapters of this book.

The chapters that follow should serve as a reminder to Christians of both their inheritance and responsibilities to serve the Lord. For nonbelievers, these biblical values should serve as guideposts for your life regardless of whether you ever accept Christ. Your family life and work life will be enhanced by adopting these values. Although there is no guarantee of financial or business success to either the believer or nonbeliever who follows these precepts, the evidence of wealthy and successful non-Christians who are ethical, honest, and diligent speaks for itself. The probability of success for anyone who follows the teachings of Christ and the Bible is greatly magnified. Of course, accepting the forgiveness of our Lord, who shed his blood on the cross, is my ultimate objective for you if you are not a Christian. I can guarantee that an eternity with Christ in heaven will provide you with real prosperity forever.

Chapter 3
A culture in Disarray

I recall in about the 2nd grade at Thomas Jefferson Public Elementary school in Baltimore, Maryland, that our class recited the Lord's Prayer every morning just after the bell rang. No one protested. No one was offended. Shortly thereafter, however, the United States Supreme Court, in the case of Engel vs. Vitale (1962), ruled that public school-sponsored prayer violated the 1st Amendment to the Constitution, establishment of religion clause. Consequently, School prayer in public schools ended in 1962.

We know that not every teacher or every student who repeated the Lord's Prayer each day was a Christian or even a believer in God. However, imagine for a moment the spiritual power of tens of millions of children's and teacher's prayers reaching up to heaven each morning. Now, consider those tens of millions of prayers for God's protection suddenly quashed.

In 1962, mass shootings in the United States were virtually unheard of. Over 60 years have passed since that Supreme Court school prayer decision.

In 2021, there were a record 692 mass shootings in the United States. Through June 5, 2022, there were 246 mass shootings in the U.S. That was the exact same number of mass shootings through June 5th in 2021. A mass shooting is defined as one where at least 4 people are shot, excluding the shooter. The number of mass shootings increased from 410 in 2019 to 610 in 2020. (www.cnn.com/2022/06/07/us/2022-shootings-pace-worst-ever/index.html; "US Mass Shootings are on pace to match last year, the worst ever, Gun Violence Data Archives Show." 6/7/22).

Is there a connection between the decline of Christianity in America with the rise of violence and criminal and immoral behavior?

Abortion was not an issue in 1962 in America. State laws in the U.S. regulated and outlawed abortion, usually after a certain number of weeks prior to birth. However, the U.S. Supreme Court, in Roe vs. Wade (1973), made access to abortion on demand virtually universal. Not until the most recent case of Dobbs vs Jackson Women's Health (2022), after almost 50 years, the power to regulate and possibly outlaw abortion once again was returned to the 50 state legislatures. In the last 49 years, tens of millions of unborn babies in the U.S. have been aborted. Some of these abortions, called partial-birth abortions, are performed literally minutes before the child is to be born.

Again, what is the relationship between the practice of abortion and the diminution of Christian faith and practice in 21st-century America?

Finally, in 2015, in Obergefell vs. Hodges (2015), the United States Supreme Court declared that a same-sex couple is endowed with a constitutional right to marry in all 50 states.

The Gallup Poll, February 2022, reflects that 7.1% of us now identify as LGBT. This is double the number recorded just 10 years ago in 2012. Furthermore, of those in Generation Z, born from 1997 to 2003, 21% self-identify as LGBT. Comedian Bill Maher recently remarked, tongue in cheek, that at that rate, by 2054, we'll all be gay! Although he remarked in jest, he certainly identified a trend in America.

These figures reflect the secularization of a culture that considers Biblical admonitions, at best, irrelevant. Should we teach our children that it really doesn't matter if they marry someone of the opposite sex or the same sex?

Finally, the divorce rate for people over 50 years of age has doubled in the last 20 years, according to research from Bowling Green University (Divorce Attitudes Among Older Adults: Two Decades of Change, Susan L. Brown, 2/27/2019, www.ncbi.nlm.nih.gov/pmc/articles/PMC6867609/).

These statistics mirror a societal and family breakdown in both the younger generation and the older generation. At the same time, violence is an out-of-control contagion in both our cities and schools. Homicide rates in U.S. cities have increased 44% just since 2019, while mass shootings are at record levels. (Homicide increased in 2021 in major American Cities, New Study finds, NicoleSganga,CBSNews,1/26/22,www.cbsnews.com/news/homicides-2021-increase-council-on-criminal-j). With the additional devastation of almost 50 years of abortion on demand, the principles of Biblical Christianity appear to have been tossed aside and deemed irrelevant by a large segment of our population today.

What can we do to reverse the moral and spiritual degeneration of our culture as individuals?

That is one of the reasons for this book. Real Prosperity presupposes a life based upon Biblical precepts.

First, we need to both pray for and provide leadership as Christians for a spiritual Bible-based revival in America. This may mean leading Bible studies, ministering to unbelievers, and participating in ministries like the "Promise Keepers" of the 1990's.

Secondly, we need to build our lives upon Biblical principles. Jesus tells us in Matthew 7:24-27, 24, "Anyone who listens to my teaching and follows it is wise, like a person who builds a house on solid rock (25). Though the rain comes in torrents and the floodwaters rise, and the winds beat against that house, it won't collapse because it is built on bedrock (26). But anyone who hears my teaching and doesn't obey it is foolish, like a person who builds a house on sand. (27)."

The twenty-one principles enunciated in this book will provide that solid rock upon which you will be able to build your house against the storms of life. You may lose a job, suffer cancer, heart disease, or lose a child to sickness or accident. Your spouse or your best friend might leave you all alone. Yet if your foundation is upon the rock of Christ, you will be safely guided past that storm.

Chapter 4
Introducing the 21 Principles that will radically revolutionize your life now.

Our society is promoting a lifestyle of video games, pornography, and marijuana for young men. Setting goals for personal success and achieving those goals is often frowned upon by hip culture. A young woman who desires marriage and children is discouraged by media promoting bisexuality, abortion, and denigration of long-term relationships in favor of job and career goals. Women today are encouraged to pursue short-term sexual relationships displayed in old TV shows such as Sex and the City.

In young men, the very essence of masculinity is undermined. Instead, young men are told that masculine behavior is "toxic" and should be shed in favor of a feminized version of what a man should look like. Establishing traditional career goals, marriage, and raising a family are deemphasized in favor of shunning traditional male leadership models and abandoning masculine character traits.

A negative attitude toward men who display an entrepreneurial spirit is also pervasive. Young men are discouraged from taking the initiative in relationships, careers, and business. Instead, they are encouraged to be passive, subservient, and slothful. Fathers are marginalized and ridiculed on television and social media. Traditional values of honesty, hard work, and faith in God are often being exchanged for an embrace of socialism, apathy, indolence, and even dishonesty.

This fundamental change in societal outlook has led to mass confusion among men and women looking for direction in a culture often resembling biblical Sodom and Gomorrah.

When I was twenty-five, I graduated from law school with a C average. Although I was about to receive a Juris Doctorate (JD) degree in law, I was single, apathetic, and directionless. I had interned for a personal injury firm in Oakland, California, and I was bored with legal research and writing legal memorandums for senior attorneys. I had no interest in practicing law whatsoever. My work ethic was poor, and I was spending too much time sleeping, watching television, and dating different women.

Just two months prior to my graduation, I responded to a recruiting ad from the FBI at my law school in San Francisco. After one meeting with a senior FBI agent, I suddenly became alive with excitement at the prospect of chasing down terrorists and bank robbers. Almost overnight, a spirit of self-discipline engulfed me. I transformed myself. First, in preparation for the final interview, I went to a San Francisco clothing store and asked the salesperson for the most conservative three-piece suit on the racks. Next, I headed for the barber to cut my lengthy locks to the shortness of a Marine Corps officer. Finally, I developed a daily fitness regimen of push-ups, sit-ups, and running to prepare for the FBI Academy at Quantico, Virginia.

My new self-discipline then spread to the California Bar Exam. Up until that time, I had been ambivalent about even taking the bar exam. California had a reputation as having the most difficult bar exam in America. The very low pass rate for the California bar was well known. My study habits in law school had been weak and erratic. At one point, I had completely stopped attending classes for six weeks simply because I was bored with law school. My C average was testimony to my apathy.

However, with my newfound goal of becoming an FBI special agent, I was now on fire to study for and pass the California Bar Exam. I immediately signed up for a six-week intensive bar review course. The classes consisted of four hours per evening of lectures. Each morning, after a two-mile run, I committed to six hours of intense study. On Saturday and Sunday, when review classes were not scheduled, I studied for eight hours each day. For the duration of that six-week period, I am convinced that I studied more than the previous three years of law school.

I was hired by the FBI in September 1978. For the next three and a half months, I underwent rigorous academics, physical fitness training, and firearms instruction at the Quantico Academy. New agents who scored less than 85 percent on the academic tests were fired. Agents who didn't qualify on the shooting range were terminated. Failure to pass physical fitness or defensive tactics tests also resulted in an agent's immediate termination. The stress level at the academy was intense.

In November, while still at the academy, I received a letter stating I had passed the California Bar Examination. From that point in my life forward, apathy, laziness, and disorganization are what I fought against. Instead, at age twenty-five, I made a decision to reorder my life with goals, self-discipline, and initiative.

Three years later, I received Christ as my personal Lord and Savior. Since then, I have strived to incorporate the twenty-one biblical principles enumerated here into my life. As with every other Christian, I am still a work in progress. Yet, with each passing year, my life more closely conforms to these principles.

***

This is not a book meant to be a quick read. Don't put this book on a shelf when you finish it. Instead, put it in your briefcase, your purse, on your coffee table, or in your coat pocket every day. Refer to one of the twenty-one steps you're on each morning five minutes after you wake up. Emblazon that step in your brain each day for seven days. For example, if you're on the generosity step, think about how you can be more generous each day for seven days. Then move to the next step. Do the same for seven days. After you complete the final step, ask your family, your friends, and your coworkers if they see a change in you. They should. Take a break for one day. Then start again at step one and go through the twenty-one steps again. If you find it difficult to see a breakthrough at any one step the first time through, double your time on that step on your second time through by spending fourteen days there. Remember, this is a lifetime process. You will never achieve perfection. It doesn't matter if you are proud of how honest or generous or kind you are. You can and always will find a way to do better the next time through. Only Jesus was perfect. He obviously didn't need this program. You do!

Make notes. As you focus on each step, write down at least one action you are taking each day to successfully complete that step. Retain your notes in a spiral notebook so you can also review them each morning as you progress.

Benjamin Franklin, the American patriot, made a list of thirteen virtues he said he worked on every day. Franklin's list included temperance, silence, order, resolution, frugality, industry, sincerity, justice, moderation, cleanliness, tranquility, and chastity (Benjamin Franklin's 13 Virtues of Success, businessinsider.com).

When he shared his list with a friend, Franklin was rankled to learn that many people thought him proud. As a result, he added humility to the list of thirteen virtues. Franklin said he worked on all thirteen values every day. Franklin's list, although not biblically based, enumerated many biblical concepts. Of course, Franklin himself was very successful. The practice of these values was important in the eighteenth century by Benjamin Franklin during the formative years of the American Revolution and shortly thereafter. This was a time of a powerful Judeo-Christian ethic, with the Bible used as a textbook in the schools and universities of that era. Certainly, today, with the prevalence of moral relativism, political correctness, and wokeism in our culture, the teaching of these biblical concepts is essential.

Will Durant summed it up perfectly:

"We are what we repeatedly do. Excellence, then, is not an act, but a habit." (https://medium.com/the-mission/my-favourite-quote-of-all-time-is-a-misattribution-66356f22843).

Ultimately, putting these twenty-one biblical concepts into practice means creating, developing, and refining twenty-one new habits. It may seem unusual to describe character qualities of honesty, hard work, kindness, and courage as "habits." However, most of us would admit that if a child is raised by parents who are engaged in crime, it is far more likely that the child becomes a criminal than the child who is raised by parents training their children to live moral lives. The habits we describe as moral are not innate. As Judeo-Christian teachings have long held, we are sinners by nature, and unless instructed otherwise, we will not naturally develop and behave as moral beings. This is not to say that you may be somewhat proficient already in mastering some of these twenty-one principles.

Let's examine the obstacles we will face in creating and building a repertoire of behaviors that will allow us to achieve the goal of real prosperity. First, since you are reading this book, we'll assume that real prosperity is a laudable goal in your view. Real prosperity, for our purposes, means that you adopt the biblical principles of moral conduct into your life. Once you have integrated these principles to the point that they become second nature, you will embark on the path of success in work, business, and family life. That path may not necessarily lead you to material wealth at the level of a multimillionaire or billionaire. It will not even guarantee you that your wife or husband will never leave you or that your children will make good choices with their lives. However, it does guarantee you the best possible opportunity for success in business, work, and family life. If, in addition, you already are or become a follower of Christ, success itself is guaranteed in your spiritual life in terms of an eternity with God. However, the principles of honesty, hard work, courage, and perseverance alone exponentially increase the probability of your success in every facet of your life, including your marriage, children, and financial blessings.

Before we identify the twenty-one qualities of character essential for true prosperity, we will describe the antonyms for each, how our culture promotes those negative qualities, and what happens when they predominate in your life. We will then describe the opposite positive quality, why it promotes success, and how to make that quality an everyday habit until it becomes part of your permanent character.

These are the twenty-one principles that will revolutionize your life. Each chapter will be devoted to one of them. For your maximum benefit, I encourage you to study them in order:

1) Faith

2) Honesty

3) Courage

4) Perseverance

5) Optimism

6) Generosity

7) Hard work

8) Obedience

9) Loyalty

10) Humility

11) Forgiveness

12) Kindness

13) Patience

14) Compassion

15) Reliability

16) Self-discipline

17) Servant leadership

18) Gratitude

19) Mentoring

20) Health and Healing

21) Freedom

Chapter 5
Week #1
Principle: FAITH

Having Faith vs. Distrust, Unbelief, and Being a Cynic

If you are cynical, you believe that most people have evil or unethical motives in their behavior toward you. "Cynicism is a feeling of dissatisfaction towards the organization, and employees believe that the organization's management lacks honesty, justice and transparency" (Omar Durrah, "Organizational Cynicism and Its Impact on Organizational Pride in Industrial Organizations," National Library of Medicine, April 3, 2019).

"It turns out that just thinking that others are mean or deceitful can have a big impact on your paycheck. . . New research published by the American Psychological Association indicates that cynicism could have a negative effect on your income over time" (Lydia Dishman, "Do Cynics Make Less Money?" Fast Company, June 3, 2015).

Recently, Olga Stavrova (Tilburg University) and Ehlebracht (University of Cologne) analyzed data from 1,146 Americans who were surveyed once and then surveyed again nine years later. They found that those who were most cynical tended to make less money. And nine years later, they still made less than idealists. Those who were least cynical just didn't do well at a moment in time. They were also on a higher trajectory of success (Brett Beasley, "Are you a Cynic? It just might Be Hurting Your Career," Notre Dame Deloitte Center for Ethical Leadership, 2022). Consequently, if you want to pursue the path to success, don't be mistrustful of your boss, your coworkers, and your business partners. Let's extrapolate this truth to your spouse and your children as well. Mistrust toward family members may create dysfunction with your loved ones and lead to divorce and juvenile delinquency.

Let's now examine the power of faith:

Principle #1: Exercise Your Faith

"Now faith is the assurance of what we hope for and the certainty of what we do not see" (Hebrews 11:1, Berean Study Bible).

Look at the thief on the cross next to Jesus. He exercised his faith in Christ when he asked the Lord to remember him when he came into his kingdom. That thief had "the certainty of what he did not see." The thief did not have an opportunity to attend church, read the Bible, or have fellowship with other Christians. He simply put his faith in Christ. Jesus promptly rewarded him when he said, "Today, you'll be with me in Paradise" (Luke 23:43).

Exercising faith is the same as seeing the glass as half full, not half empty. A person of a simple faith conveys a positive attitude to others that is infectious. Faith gives birth to perseverance, self-discipline, and victory over our fears. Because we have faith in the ultimate positive outcome, we can sustain perseverance in difficulties and self-discipline in the face of temporary pain. We defeat our fears based on our knowledge that, in the end, based on our faith, we win!

"And Jesus answered them, 'Have faith in God. Truly, I say to you, whoever says to this mountain, "Be taken up and thrown into the sea," and does not doubt in his heart but believes that what he says will come to pass, it will be done for him. Therefore, I tell you, 'Whatever you ask in prayer, believe that you have received it, and it will be yours'" (Mark 11:22–24).

The message here is not to try to toss the Rocky Mountains out to the Pacific Ocean! Rather, what seems impossible to you and me in the natural is not only possible, but plausible with God. Everyone knows and loves the underdog. American farmers with muskets defeated England, the greatest empire in the world, in 1776. The US hockey team upset Russia in the 1980 Olympics. Martin Luther King Jr. overcame racism and the Ku Klux Klan to establish civil rights for African Americans. Men and women rise from poverty to build billion-dollar businesses across America. The "can do" attitude upon which America is anchored reflects faith in our ability to overcome incredible odds to achieve success. As a Christian, I marshal my faith and confidence in God. A nonbeliever might base his or her faith simply upon confidence in self. When you listen to people who constantly tell you all the reasons they and you will not succeed, they are devoid of faith in God, self, or you. Avoid those people (unless, of course, they happen to be your spouse or children!). If you are, unfortunately, working under a boss with a negative attitude, you may want to seek a job transfer or look for other employment. The negative attitudes of bosses and others will eventually drag you down unless you consciously fight for a faith-based positive outlook each day.

Regarding business, "having a positive attitude opens your mind to trying new methods, adapting to new technologies, and identifying opportunities." According to research conducted by NCBI, National Center for Biotechnology Information, people with a positive mindset are more successful because they recognize opportunities and take advantage of them ("Why Having a Positive Attitude Matters if You Want to Succeed," Digital Resource, www.yourdigitalresource.com/post/having-a-positive-attitude-matters).

If we're caught up in thinking that we will probably fail and visualizing worst-case scenarios in our job or business, how can we expect to focus our minds on new opportunities? A negative thinker fears a promotion. Who can focus on being promoted if they're obsessed already with failure in their current job, project, or business?

As believers, we realize that often, the temptation to be afraid is itself a spiritual attack upon our minds. Your resistance and belief in your eventual success also may be a godly spiritual response to that temptation. As the Bible indicates in Ephesians 6:12, "For our struggle is not against flesh and blood, but against the rulers, against the authorities, against the powers of this dark world and against the spiritual forces of evil in the heavenly realms."

Remember, fear and faith will always remain diametrically opposed to each other. Increase the amount of time meditating on your faith in a positive future. Reduce the habit of fear with the goal of eliminating it from your life.

Exercise Your Faith: Actions for Follow-Up.

Week 1

#1: When have you exercised faith in the past, and the outcome was positive for you? Do you see yourself as a person with a positive or a negative attitude? When has your failure to display faith resulted in a disappointment, a loss, or a total disaster? Are you refusing to be positive and faithful about your future because you don't want to be disappointed?

#2: In what projects, jobs, or promotions can you start exercising faith now? For example, do you want a promotion or pay raise? You will need to see yourself receiving the new position and performing it well. At home, do you want better relations with your spouse or children? Start exercising faith in God so that you can affect these relationships and improve them. Also, have faith in yourself that you can develop better relationships at home and at work.

#3: What obstacles are in the way of your having faith? Have you been a negative thinker most of your life? This will be a matter of discarding the habit of negative thinking and exchanging it for faith and a positive outlook. Make a list of what advantages you see in retaining a negative outlook on life. Next to each item, describe why these "advantages" are really disadvantages. For instance, many people feel that by maintaining a negative outlook, they won't be disappointed by a negative outcome. If they're applying for a job, they see themselves being rejected. However, by anticipating the failure outcome, they are psychologically preventing themselves from approaching the job interview with confidence and swagger. The man of faith, by contrast, walks into the interview brimming with confidence that he will be the one hired. His projection of positivity, enthusiasm, and candor is like a big red sign flashing, "Hire me. I can do this."

#4: What sacrifices will you need to make in order to engage your faith in God and yourself in order to be successful? Do you need to give up your shield of negative thinking that is protecting you from your fear of disappointment? Do you view acquiring faith in God and belief in yourself as a "sacrifice" for you?

#5: If you continue without faith and self-confidence in ten years, will you regret that you're still mired in negative thinking and failure in your career, your business, and your family relationships? Think of yourself as a person faithful to God and confident in your abilities for the next ten years and what you might accomplish.

#6: Rise up in your faith and confidence today. Select one important goal from day #2 that will require extreme faith in God and self to accomplish. Go for it! (If it is a longer-term goal such as a job promotion, what one step can you take today toward achieving that objective?)

#7: Say a prayer today. Ask God to fill you with the faith of King David facing Goliath. Meditate upon confidence in yourself and faith in your abilities driving you to succeed.

Chapter 6
Week #2
Principle: HONESTY

Honesty vs. Dishonesty

Among the best indicators of the acceptance of dishonesty in our culture today are the statistics on lying in America. Most people lie on average four times each day. The most common reasons for lying include:

1. To save face.

2. To shift blame.

3. To avoid confrontation.

4. To get one's way.

5. To be nice.

6. To make yourself feel better.

(Brandon Gaille, "Small Business & Marketing Advice," www.brandongaille.com)

Dishonesty has become rampant in our culture today. Lying has become as American as apple pie. Unlike for Covid or the flu, wearing a mask and social distancing won't prevent you from getting caught up in the epidemic. Only conscious, intentional behavior on a daily basis will protect you from this infection.

Dishonesty in business today takes many forms.

In the workplace, dishonesty may take the form of stealing a $20 bill from the register by the cashier. Or the employee with responsibility for company funds may embezzle money for himself or a bank teller might pocket some of the Bank's cash while she's working the drive through window. A purchasing agent may take a bribe in exchange for selecting the supplier who bribes him. A salesclerk at a clothing store steals a new dress. A government employee calls in sick, uses paid leave, when she just wants to go to the beach. In the white-collar corporate world, pharmaceutical companies have advertised prescription drugs as "safe," while knowing full well they cause cancer. Senior citizens are routinely defrauded by telemarketers selling them worthless products.

We are awash in dishonest business practices today. However, the upshot of dishonest practices is the lack of blessing. Generally, most dishonesty is traceable by police or other law enforcement. Eventually, the perpetrator(s) are discovered and usually prosecuted. Even if you are not eventually discovered, the guilt and shame of your unethical or illegal conduct may be overwhelming. Finally, the blessing of God is absent.

Ultimately, dishonesty brings short term gain in exchange for long term shame!

Principle #2: Honesty: Without It, Nothing Else Matters

"Honesty guides good people; dishonesty destroys treacherous people" (Proverbs 11:3).

"One who is faithful in a very little is also faithful in much, and one who is dishonest in a very little is also dishonest in much" (Luke 16:10).

How many businesspeople and how many companies have been destroyed by dishonesty? Lack of integrity is rampant in America today." In a recent survey of US retailers, about 69 percent of stores said they have seen an increase in organized theft in the past year" ("Robberies are becoming an increasing concern for Retailers,"

NYTimes.com, November 26, 2021). "Flash mob" robberies are shocking large and small shop owners alike and traumatizing their employees." Experts say the brazen crimes, which can involve dozens of thieves carrying weapons and breaking glass, are likely being coordinated on social media apps" ("Flash Mob Robberies Roiling U.S. Retailers, traumatizing Workers, Washington Post, December 3, 2021). Victims include Nordstrom, Best Buy, Louis Vuitton, and Home Depot, among others.

In the US, ten million Americans were victimized by identity theft in the last year (Federal Trade Commission).

Whether it's cheating on taxes, lying on a job application, or taking home company supplies for your personal use, white collar dishonesty is also overwhelming our culture today.

The biblical axiom "One who is dishonest in a very little is also dishonest in much" still stands true today. If the barista at Starbucks accidentally gives you one dollar more in change when you buy a mocha, you should, of course, immediately give it back. If you don't, you may think of it as no big deal. The Starbucks corporation won't miss the dollar. Starbucks stock won't go down, and certainly no one will know you pocketed an extra dollar. However, if you're in a position in your job to gain an extra $25,000 dishonestly and no one will know the difference, will you behave any differently? Probably not. Either you have established the habit and discipline of personal integrity, or you haven't.

If you make an error at work, do you immediately start thinking about how you can cover it up without anyone knowing the difference? Or do you go to your supervisor and report it?

If you're traveling out of town on business, do you falsely inflate your expenses for your company expense report where no one will find out anyway?

If your boss asks you how the project is going, do you say, "Everything's fine," when you know there's a problem? Or do you describe the problem and ask for assistance or more time to complete the job?

If your husband or wife asks you why you're late getting home from work, do you create an excuse about heavy traffic? Or do you tell the truth: "I stopped for a drink with my coworkers"?

A life that reflects personal integrity will make you stand out in your office and your company and make you a role model for your children. Again, there is no guarantee that you'll be promoted simply because you are scrupulously honest. However, a high level of personal integrity is essential whether you want to be promoted or own the business and you want your employees to see you setting an example for them.

Do you compartmentalize honesty? A salesman may be kind, considerate, and honest with his customers while he lies and cheats upon his wife at home. We can be Dr. Jekyll and Mr. Hyde in different roles in our lives. We need to examine honesty at work, at home, and in our business dealings. I noted a few years ago that I was often impatient, combative, and downright nasty when dealing with customer service agents on the phone when I called about errors on my cell phone bill. Of course, it doesn't help when you've been overcharged, placed on hold for twenty minutes, transferred to two or three different agents, and finally hung up on. However, frustrated, I would call back angry and yell at the innocent person who had the misfortune of answering my call. So, I was forced to decompartmentalize my own outrageous behavior and exercise some patience and kindness.

Honesty: Actions for Follow-Up, Week #2

#1: In what areas of your work life are you not being completely honest?

(a) Review your relationship with your boss.

Have you ever hidden information from him or her that might reflect unfavorably on you?

(b) Are you honest with your subordinates?

If your subordinates and coworkers were asked, would they describe you as a very honest person?

(c) If someone were watching you all day at work, would they be able to see lack of integrity in any part of your workday?

In what areas of your home life are you not being completely honest?

(d) Focus on your relationship with your husband or wife.

Are you truthful with your spouse in all things?

Are you totally faithful to your spouse?

Do you hide any bills from your wife or husband because you don't want them to know you incurred them?

Have you secretly put money aside that your spouse doesn't know about?

(e) Review your relationships with your children.

Are you truthful with your kids?

Would your kids describe you as an honest dad or mom?

#2: Think of instances when it was difficult to be honest, you were honest anyway, and it paid off for you. Make a list of these instances and how it felt to be honest when nobody would know the difference if you had lied. As a believer, you know that you will be blessed for your integrity. Your good character is a positive witness to your employer, your business associates, and your family.

#3: What obstacles are impeding you from being more honest? For example, you may fear that your customers may not patronize your company if they knew certain aspects of your business. You may fear telling your boss that you are behind on your work because you fear his or her wrath.

#4: What sacrifices will you need to make to be more honest with your boss, your customers, and your spouse? For example, you may need to surrender a false image you have created at work or with your spouse. A frank conversation admitting your mistakes can be a major but needed sacrifice for your ego.

#5: If you continue to be dishonest with your employer, your business associates, your customers, or your spouse, how will your life look in one year, five years, ten years? Will you be unemployed, possibly divorced, or alone?

#6: Where can you be honest at work today? For example, how can you more honestly relate to your boss, coworkers, customers, and spouse today?

#7: Ask the Lord to help you overcome any tendency to be less than truthful.

Chapter 7
Week #3
Principle: COURAGE

Courage vs. Cowardice

"Hire salespeople who are really smart problem solvers, but lack courage, hunger and competitiveness, and your company will go out of business" (Ben Horowitz, Top 60 Ben Horowitz Quotes, 2022, quote fancy. com).

Don't risk putting a cowardly person in charge of your nation, team, office, company, or family. Cowardly leaders will say what they think people want to hear because they're afraid to speak the truth. Your whole company is put in jeopardy if your chief financial officer is painting a picture of growing revenues and profits when the business is hemorrhaging cash.

The cowardly leader won't make a hard decision. If the company needs to expand locations to grow the business, the cowardly leader will fear investing the added capital and taking the risk that the expansion may not work. In the Civil War, President Lincoln repeatedly was frustrated because his commanding general refused to take the risk of attacking the Southern army even though the North enjoyed numerical superiority and overwhelming firepower. Consequently, Lincoln fired several generals because they lacked the courage to launch an offensive against the South. Finally, he appointed General Ulysses Grant. General Grant immediately initiated a full-scale offensive, eventually resulting in the capture of Richmond and winning the war.

Cowardly leaders will take the path of least resistance. When there is a need for change, a cowardly leader is unwilling to take the risk of taking a position that is not popular. Martin Luther King Jr. was arrested twenty-nine times protesting racial segregation and discrimination in the South. The majority of Americans in that era were appalled at the civil rights leader's audacity to challenge their worldview.

Principle #3, Courage – Be Courageous

The Bible describes the need for us to be brave: "Be strong and courageous. Do not be afraid or terrified because of them, for the Lord your God goes with you; he will never leave you nor forsake you" (Deuteronomy 31:6–8).

In Psalm 56:6–8, David states, "When I am afraid, I put my trust in you." David would later become Israel's king and is described "as a man after God's own heart" (1 Samuel 13:14).

Note that David admits he is afraid. However, he puts his trust in God so he can be courageous. David does not say that he is fearless. The difference is this: We are all afraid of many things. We may fear failure in our job or a project we need to complete. We may fear sickness and disease. Or we may fear our boss or not having enough money to retire or to put our children through college. However, God is not requiring David or you to never be afraid. God is telling us to go forward despite our fears and place our trust in him. So, take that job and save for your retirement and your kids' college education. Trust God to heal you of your sickness.

Even if you are not a believer, the key is to go forward with the job, the saving of your money, the medical treatment the doctor prescribes, regardless of the fear you are experiencing. The important point is not to berate yourself simply because you are afraid. No one is fearless. When the soldier in battle heroically charges an enemy machine gun despite a high risk of death, he is acting "courageously," not "fearlessly." If he were to charge the machine gun without any fear (fearlessly), there would be no need for courage. Consequently, when you feel your stomach churn, when your palms are sweaty, and when your mouth is dry, don't let that stop you from going into the boss's office and asking for that raise!

The lack of courage is probably the most common character flaw preventing success in a job, a business, and a marriage, and in raising children.

Millions of people develop great ideas and plans to start new businesses every day. They're excited. They pitch their ideas for a new coffee shop, online furniture website, McDonald's franchise, or stock investment opportunity. Their spouse, friends, and coworkers listen attentively. Then the husband says, "How are we going to pay for this?" or the wife shakes her head and says, "It's too risky. You'll lose our retirement." The would-be entrepreneur walks away sadly and never broaches the bold plan for success ever again. We are often afraid to pursue our goals because of the criticism of those close to us whom we love and respect. We see our sweaty palms and churning stomach as a red flag saying, "Stop. Give up now."

Courage is simply acknowledging our fear and moving forward anyway. Moving forward can be based on our confidence in God, faith in our own ability, and/or simply a dogged determination to succeed. Never believe you must be "fearless" before stepping out and taking action. Instead, shout, "Yes, I can, and I will do it!" (Go in your office and lock the door first. We don't want your coworkers to think you've completely lost it!) Uttering those words and starting up the hill is courage. Nike's slogan "Just do it" is always appropriate when we encounter fear.

Many years ago, psychologist Dr. James Dobson wrote the book, "Dare to Discipline," (1970). Dobson's thesis is that when your kids misbehave and defy you, you must have the courage to discipline them. Otherwise, you will find yourself raising rebellious teenagers who will be getting in trouble at school and with the law.

In marriage or in any close friendship, we are called upon to be open and reveal our innermost feelings to our partner. Hiding our hurt feelings or resentments or keeping secrets from our partner can only be destructive of the relationship. Again, courage is front and center. We must take action to get past our great fear of rejection by our spouse or partner.

Procrastination is often a reflection of great fear. We postpone acting because we fear the consequences more than we embrace the hoped-for outcome. Adolf Hitler was successful in conquering one European nation after another because the leaders of England and France feared the consequences of ordering him to stop early on. As a result, Hitler was able to build up his forces and aggressively steamroll over cities and nations before England finally declared war. By that time, Hitler had amassed a huge army, enslaved many nations, causing the deaths of millions of people because the leaders who could have stopped him were afraid to act.

Have you ever been afraid to ask the boss for a raise? Then, when you muster the courage to request it, there's an awkward silence. That's usually because the boss is surprised and may be fearful of turning you down because he or she can't risk your leaving the company! Whether the boss grants your request or not, you'll be proud of yourself for being brave enough to ask. Many of your coworkers will lack courage. You will gain both the pay raise and the self-esteem boost because you had the courage to ask and risk rejection.

Risk-Taking: The Requirement of Courage

What do starting a new business, buying a franchise, or accepting a new job a thousand miles away from your home all have in common? They are risk taking events requiring courage. Yet they are potential pathways to unlimited success and to earning millions of dollars. However, most Americans will never start businesses, buy franchises, or take new jobs far away from their home and family. You may be the most honest, hardworking, kind, humble, and highly intelligent employee. However, if you cannot train yourself in the habit of courage, you will never accomplish much in your career. People less intelligent, `prideful, often unkind, and with less integrity than you will probably be your boss.

Now, you may tell me that you aren't interested in starting a business and you don't wish to move a thousand miles away from family. That's fine. However, even if you wish to remain with the same company, if you want to get promoted or get a better job, you still must exhibit courage.

When I was 30 years old, I was appointed as the Executive Assistant Superintendent of the Oregon State Police, at the rank of Major. This was an exciting high-level position with a large state agency. I was tasked with being the chief legal and policy advisor to the Superintendent. My duties included testifying before the legislature on pending legislation, negotiating labor contracts, and representing the agency at various events. However, the executive staff were older men in their 50's and 60's. There was resentment among several of the senior staff against a new 30-year-old boss instructing them to change their policies to conform to new legal requirements. Their resentment of my oversight of their work resulted in criticism and many challenges to my authority. The stress of the position caused me to be fearful that the Superintendent did not approve of my performance. I gradually became anxious, depressed, and I suffered from panic attacks. However, I was too afraid to sit down and discuss my concerns with the Superintendent. Instead, concluding that I was at a dead end in my job, I resigned and returned to my law practice. I felt discouraged and defeated.

Just three weeks after returning to my law practice, I was informed that the Superintendent was deeply disappointed in my resignation. In fact, he was planning to promote me to the rank of Colonel the following year. This would have cleared a path for me to eventually rise to become Superintendent. Despite my perceived stress, I actually enjoyed the job. Had I known that the Superintendent was extremely pleased with my work, I would not have been saddled with anxiety, depression, and panic attacks. However, my lack of the simple courage to sit down with my boss and confront my fears had cost me unbearable stress and the loss of a career with the agency. Fortunately, I went on to a very successful career in law and later as a stockbroker and investment manager. However, I had learned a hard lesson in the necessity of courage.

A few years ago, a friend encouraged me to run for the position of treasurer of the Oregon Republican Party. I had never previously held office in any political party. The candidate for state party chairman asked me to be his running mate as the candidate for state party treasurer. I agreed. On the date of the election by the party's central committee, he was soundly defeated in the vote for state chairman. An aide to the new party chairman then approached me prior to the vote for the party treasurer. The aide told me that since my candidate for party chairman had lost badly, as his running mate, I had zero chance of winning the party treasurer position. He said I would ruin my political career and look silly by losing in a landslide. I feared that I would lose badly and be humiliated. Despite my fear, I felt that the Lord wanted me to run and that we needed more Christians in these positions. So, I responded to the aide by saying, "What political career? I don't have one anyway." I stayed in the race and won the party election by one vote. Truly, the Lord was blessing my courage in the face of my fears.

I cannot overemphasize the importance of acquiring this habit. Courage will serve you in business, family, church, and when you retire. You can't effectively serve God, your country, your community, or your spouse without it.

Courage: Actions for Follow-Up, Week #3

#1: Where are you being intimidated at your work or your business?

a) Are you afraid to ask for help with a project when you need it?

b) Do you fear asking for feedback from your boss by asking him or her how you can perform your job better and what your areas of critical weakness are?

c) When you have an opportunity for a new assignment or promotion, do you shy away because you fear making mistakes or being overwhelmed?

d) If you have your own business, do you fear expanding your company because you might not have sufficient funds or go broke?

e) Do you fear correcting your employees when they make mistakes because they might quit, or you might be perceived as a bad boss?

#2: Analyze what you fear the most, that is preventing you from being more successful at work or growing your business.

a) How do you overcome that fear now?

You will overcome that fear simply by doing what you fear.

b) Start out with baby steps in overcoming these fears. For example, if you own a business and fear the risk of going broke by opening new stores, slow down your growth plan and focus all your energy on opening just one new location instead of three. Build more slowly.

c) If you fear taking on a new assignment at work or a job promotion, be committed to studying all the tasks of the new project or new job. Ask for help. Then dedicate all your efforts to making it work.

In summary, don't let yourself off the hook with your excuses for being afraid. Remember how hard it was to think of being able to drive a car before you received your license. It is the same with a new job.

Often the difference between the guy working in the supply room and the CEO is simply that the CEO, while acknowledging that he or she was afraid, persisted in pushing through sweaty palms and a quaking voice to take the promotions and tackle the new challenges every step of the way. By contrast, the supply room clerk remained in his comfort zone, never nervous but never successful.

#3: What are the obstacles for you to overcome your fears? Obstacles might include embarrassment and humiliation if you step out with courage and fail.

#4: What sacrifices will you need to make to defeat these fears? Perhaps you fear failure. So, you may need to be willing to accept the fact that your actions may not succeed initially and simply realize that if that happens, you will try again. The sacrifice for success may be two or three failures along the way.

#5: Ask yourself, "How will I feel in one year, five years, and ten years if I am unwilling to step out courageously and try to succeed? What will my self-esteem look like in five years if I don't show courage now?"

#6: Show your badge of courage! Step out and take action! Whether the action you take results in success or not, congratulate yourself for stepping up to the plate and showing courage. Each time you step out courageously will make it a little easier the next time. Courage becomes a habit that will spread like wildfire throughout every area of your life.

#7: Thank God for the courage to go forward and take action. God loves you and will be proud of you regardless of whether you succeed. God always applauds and ultimately will reward our courage.

Chapter 8
Week #4
Principle: PERSEVERANCE

Persevering vs. Timidity and Indecision

You'll never grow your business unless you promote it. If you're timid, you won't take the initiative, and you will be left behind.

When I was 36, I was engaged in the general practice of law in the small community of Shelton, Washington. In a small town, the lawyer must be a generalist to survive. You can be a "jack of all trades, but master of none." In other words, to financially succeed, I needed to be able to defend criminals, help people divorce, and manage the distribution of an estate when my client died. I would also handle personal injury litigation when someone was injured in an auto accident, or they had a complaint against Walmart because they slipped and fell in a store. I was bored, stressed, and working long hours as an attorney trying to be a "master" of many areas of the law. However, financially, my family and I were enjoying a stable income.

My cousin, three thousand miles away, in Baltimore, had been a financial advisor and manager for Merrill Lynch investments for many years. In a conversation with him, I told him that I was dissatisfied with my small-town law practice and that I would like to explore a different opportunity. My cousin touted the high income and more relaxed lifestyle he was enjoying as a financial advisor and investment broker. However, he cautioned me that only approximately 5% of the people who become financial advisors survive the first five years in the business. I, of course, asked him why. My cousin told me that the position was 100% commission based and most new advisors become discouraged and give up because it generally takes two to three years to build a clientele and a decent income. During those first couple years, you would generally need to make 40 or 50 cold calls per day asking people to buy a stock or bond from you. These would be people who you were ideally calling from a list of people who at least were ostensibly wealthy. At worst, you might need to start calling out of the white pages of what then was the phone book. Most of the people you call would not be interested in purchasing any investments from you. Many of the people you called would either curse you out or simply hang up on you before you finished talking.

In addition, my cousin advised me that even after persisting in the making of all these calls, you might not be cut out for the financial investment business. With all your perseverance, you still may fail.

However, he did add that once you completed the gauntlet of cold calls in two or three years and managed to build a base of clientele, you would no longer need to cold call anyone. You would receive referrals from your clients, you would enjoy a six-figure income and be able to take at least five to six weeks of vacation each year. In essence, I would be my own boss.

At last, my cousin stated the obvious. In order to land among the 5% of Financial Advisors to survive and thrive, I needed to embrace two-character qualities or habits. First, I must be courageous enough to step out from my financially comfortable law practice. Secondly, I needed to commit to persevering in this business for at least two to three years regardless of the weeks and months when I received little income and much cussing out! As I mulled over making this change, I also understood that self-discipline would also be imperative if I was to succeed. I would need to do the things I did not like to do in order to achieve the goal which I desired.

Finally, one more character quality would be needed, humility. I would need to be humble enough to accept a lower income for the next two years and the change from an established attorney to a rookie financial advisor.

Fortunately, I made the change at the ripe old age of 37 and went on to a very successful career as a financial advisor. However, without the application of the biblical principles of perseverance, courage, Self-discipline, and humility, I would be just another unhappy lawyer!

"Action is often the difference between success and failure. In a comprehensive study of 17,000 executives, decisiveness—making decisions quickly—mattered significantly more than the quality of those decisions. Too often, leaders delay decisions or worse, make none at all." (Johanna Wise, "Leadership Flaws: Indecision Is a Bad Decision," Forbes, October 29, 2019).

What is the main reason for indecision? Fear. When you are paralyzed by fear, it is impossible to take action to solve your problem. The result is failure.

Eastman Kodak had been the global leader in camera film in the twentieth century. In 1975, a Kodak engineer invented the first digital camera. However, Kodak management viewed the filmless camera as a threat to their dominance in the film industry. Their executives were indecisive in taking advantage of the opportunity to revolutionize their marketplace with the sale of digital cameras instead of film. Soon digital cameras supplanted cameras requiring film. Consequently, in 2012, Kodak declared bankruptcy due to the indecisiveness and fear of its leaders.

Why did Blockbuster Video fail? In 2004, Blockbuster was America's leader in video rentals. They even had the foresight to evolve from the old VHS tapes to DVDs. However, with the advent of Netflix and later streaming services, Blockbuster was too timid to grasp the new opportunities in streaming and mailing DVDs to customers. Consequently, they were compelled to close all but one of their stores as customers turned away from their brick-and-mortar stores (Katrina Aaslaid, "50 Examples of Corporations That Failed to Innovate," Valuer, July 2, 2019).

Principle #4: Perseverance

"And let us not grow weary of doing good, for in due season we will reap, if we do not give up. As for you, brothers, do not grow weary in doing good. For you have need of endurance, so that when you have done the will of God you may receive what is promised. But the one who endures to the end will be saved" (Galatians 6:9, ESV).

You will get absolutely zero value from reading this book without perseverance and tenacity. By practicing the twenty-one values enumerated here daily for the rest of your life, you will be nothing less than one of the strongest people in your circle.. Three great examples of perseverance: the Apostle Paul, Abraham Lincoln, and Benjamin Franklin.

The Apostle Paul was determined to preach the Gospel everywhere he felt God was leading him. Paul was repeatedly arrested, jailed, and harassed by religious leaders, and later beaten within an inch of his life. Yet despite continual threats to his life, he persevered until he was later imprisoned and beheaded. In spite of his fate, he wrote approximately one half of the New Testament, bringing millions of people worldwide to Christ.

Abraham Lincoln, who may be our greatest president, displayed remarkable determination and perseverance in the face of failure. Born in 1809, he lost his job at age twenty-three and lost the business he started a year later in 1833. Three years later, the young lady to whom he was engaged to marry died. Lincoln suffered a nervous breakdown. Two years Later, Lincoln was defeated in a race for speaker of the Illinois House of Representatives. In 1843, Lincoln lost again in a contest for his party's nomination for a congressional seat. Finally, in 1846, Lincoln was elected to Congress. However, just three years later, he was rejected in a bid for land officer, and in 1854 he lost an election for the US Senate. Two years later, he lost a bid for the US vice presidential nomination, and in 1858, he was once again defeated in a Senate race.

Yet Lincoln was persevering and tenacious. In just two more years, in 1860, he was elected President of the United States on the eve of the Civil War (www.Quozio.com, 2022).

Finally, Benjamin Franklin, one of America's Founding Fathers, was so disciplined that he focused every day on one of his listed virtues in order to change and improve his own character and become the successful patriot and inventor we know him as today.

Tenacity is more than endurance; it is endurance combined with the absolute certainty that what we are looking for is going to transpire (Oswald Chambers, My Utmost for His Highest, 1935).

There is a difference between tenacity and persistence. Both persistence and tenacity are laudable character qualities, and both may lead to eventual success. However, the persistent man submits his resume to one employer after another. He may send his resume to 500 different employers before a company calls him for an interview. On the other hand, after four or five rejections, the tenacious man calls his mentor and advisors and may ask, "How can I be more successful in obtaining job interviews by modifying my resume?" This man then amends his resume to make it more appealing to potential employers. After another 10 submissions, he is called in for an interview.

Before becoming "Colonel Sanders," Harland Sanders submitted his now world-famous fried chicken recipe to 1,009 restaurants before finding a buyer. If he had not, today we would not have Kentucky Fried Chicken!

Elvis Presley also faced rejection with a determined attitude. Before becoming a household name, Elvis was fired by Jimmy Denny, then manager of Nashville's Grand Ole Opry after one show, saying, "You ain't goin' nowhere, son. You ought to go back to drivin' a truck" ("10 Famous People Who Proved That Perseverance Pays Off," Web Essentials, www.verizon.com/business/small-business-essentials/resources/for-most-of-us-success-is-one-of-our-biggest-career/).

The conviction that you will attain your goals can overcome deficiencies in skill, intellect, and knowledge.

Perseverance and Tenacity: Actions for Follow-Up, Week #6

#1: Look at your past. When have you displayed perseverance in the past to achieve a goal? When have you given up on a project or goal because you found it too difficult to achieve? Did you lack tenacity when you gave up on a goal? In other words, were you unwilling to seek counsel as to how you might change your methodology to achieve that goal? Make a list of your successes and your failures.

#2: Determine your three most important goals for the next five years. List all the benefits of achieving these goals. What would your life be like if you accomplished these goals? Of course, five-year goals will require your perseverance. If you are going to be tenacious, how might you need to modify your methods in order to achieve your goals?

#3: What actions can you take daily to accomplish these three goals? These may include taking classes, investing money in a mutual fund, taking steps to improve your work performance, or other actions that move you closer and closer to your objectives.

#4: What obstacles are impeding the achievement of your three goals? List them on paper, and then next to each obstacle, enumerate how you will overcome it. For example, how might you address lack of funds? Can you get a loan, a higher-paying job, or a more aggressive investment portfolio?

#5: Identify what you are willing to sacrifice to achieve your three goals. When I decided to lose weight, increase my energy level, and improve my health, I set a goal of running two miles per day, seven days a week. Immediately, I realized that the best way for me to make sure I accomplished this goal every day was to run two miles every morning before I did anything else. Consequently, I would be required to wake up at least forty-five minutes earlier than usual. That was the sacrifice I would make daily. I made that decision when I was twenty-three years old. I have been running at least two miles a day ever since with the rare exception of when there is so much ice and snow on the ground that it would not be safe to run. If I have an early morning meeting at my office on a given day, I make certain to run that evening. This is a positive addiction, born of my perseverance and personal tenacity. You can do the same in whatever sphere of your life you choose.

#6: If you surrender your goals because they appear to be too difficult, time-consuming, or not worth the bother, will you regret giving up the effort next year, in five years, or later life? If the answer is yes, reassess. Review the benefits of achieving your goals and how wonderful you will feel when they are met. Also, your personal self-esteem will increase when you take pride in your self-discipline as you work to fulfill your dreams. Remember, most folks don't set any goals, and of those who do, it is rare for them to possess the self-discipline to achieve them.

#7: If you're a Christian, pray for a minimum of ten minutes each day for the Holy Spirit to direct you in setting your goals and achieving them.

"An example of cynicism is when you always see the worst and have a hard time seeing the good in anyone" (www.yourdictionary.com).

Chapter 9
Week #5
Principle: OPTIMISM

Being Hopeful and Optimistic vs. Being Pessimistic, Anxious and Depressed

Pessimists are specialists in visualizing the worst-case scenarios as their personal reality. If a pessimist wins the million-dollar lottery, he immediately envisions the federal and state taxes he must pay. He foresees his wife, his kids, his uncles, his aunts, and his cousins besieging him with requests for money. He thinks the IRS will audit him, accuse him of not paying some taxes, and put him in jail. Also, he knows that he now has enough money to retire even though he's only forty-five years old. However, he read somewhere that people who suddenly retire early without another business or hobby often get sick and die. Finally, he was warned by a friend that many people who win the lottery are overwhelmed with their new wealth, spend themselves in oblivion, and go broke. So, he sees himself in jail, broke or dead!

"Staying optimistic may help you live longer and better than your more pessimistic counterparts. Researchers from Boston University came to that conclusion after following 233 men over 22 years. They reported that the study participants who had a more optimistic attitude had higher levels of emotional well-being and experienced stress differently and less frequently than those who were more pessimistic" (Christopher Curley, "Optimists Tend to Live Longer, Study Says," www.healthline.com, March 10, 2022).

Also, "viewing the glass as half full may be the secret to a longer life, according to a US study that found a positive correlation between levels of optimism and longevity. Conducted by Boston University School of Medicine, the study found that optimists not only live longer in general but have a better chance than pessimists of reaching the age of 85 and older" (Emma Tyrrell, City A.M., "Glass Half Full: Optimists Outlive Pessimists, Study Finds," City A.M., August 27, 2019).

Perpetually expecting the worst-case scenario to play out in your life will lead you to cigarettes, alcohol, and drugs to quell your fears and anxieties.

Principle #5: Hope, Optimism

"Beloved, I pray that you may prosper in all things and be in health, just as your soul prospers" (3 John 1:2).

This verse is not about "name it and claim it." It is about maintaining a positive attitude of hope and faith. For a Christian, our source of hope and optimism, of course, is faith in Christ.

Recent studies reinforce this view: "Optimism is a lucrative investment beyond one's finances. Optimists do better over the course of their careers as well. They make more money and are more likely to be promoted. . . . A landmark study by research partner Dr. Martin Seligman from the University of Pennsylvania found that optimistic sales professionals outsell their pessimistic counterparts by 56%" (Michelle Gielan, "The Financial Upside of Being an Optimist," Harvard Business Review, March 12, 2019).

Retaining hope and faith is all about attitude. For the nonbeliever, it may be the words of Dr. Karl Menninger, who said:

"Attitudes are more important than facts." That is worth repeating until its truth grips you. Any fact facing us, however difficult, even seemingly hopeless, is not as important as our attitude toward that fact. How you think about a fact may defeat you before you ever do anything about it. You may permit a fact to overwhelm you mentally before you start to deal with it factually. On the other hand, a confident and optimistic thought pattern can modify or overcome the fact altogether." (www.centreforoptimism.com/Quotes-from-The-Power-of-Positive-Thinking-by-Norman-Vincent-Peale)

The key to greater self-esteem, more energy, and the ability to work harder is found in a positive mental attitude.

"Walt Disney was fired from his first job at the Kansas City Star after his newspaper editor told him that he didn't have enough imagination or creativity. A few years later, he drove Disney's animation studio, Laugh-O-Gram, into bankruptcy. Only when he moved to California to produce cartoons did his career ultimately take off. Walt Disney's determination to meet his goals is a great example of overcoming life's obstacles" (Familius LLC, 2020, www.familius.com)

"Jim (James Eugene) Carrey, the actor, had more than one challenge in his growing years. He found out at a very early age that he had dyslexia, which created a barrier for him in school. He struggled to support his mother in her battle with severe depression. And he also had to move to Toronto, Canada, in his teen years, living with his family in their Volkswagen camper for the first eight months of their residency. Barriers presented themselves, but Carrey prevailed. In an interview with Oprah Winfrey in 1997, Carrey shares one of his largest bouts of adversity and how he used positive affirmations and visualization techniques to conquer it ("What Oprah Learned from Jim Carrey," Oprah's Life Class, Oprah Winfrey Network, YouTube video, February 17, 1997, (interview).

Both Jim Carrey and Walt Disney used hope and optimism to overcome extreme personal obstacles to achieve eventual success.

One of the best examples of optimism in the Bible is the story of David and Goliath. No one in the Israeli army was willing to fight the eight-foot giant. When sixteen-year-old David, with no military experience, stepped forward, King Saul said, "Don't be ridiculous. There's no way you can fight this Philistine and possibly win! You're only a boy, and he's been a man of war since his youth'" (1 Samuel 17:33).

However, David replied, "'I have been taking care of my father's sheep and goats,' he said. 'When a lion or a bear comes to steal a lamb from the flock, I go after it with a club and rescue the lamb from its mouth. If the animal turns on me, I catch it by the jaw and club it to death. I have done this to both lions and bears, and I'll do it to this pagan Philistine, too, for he has defied the armies of the living God! The Lord who rescued me from the claws of the lion and the bear will rescue me from this Philistine!" (1 Samuel 17:34–37).

David, the optimist, and young man of courage was right!

Will positive thinking always work? Absolutely not. I'm 5'9" and 160 lbs. in my sixties. I may want to play defensive end for the Baltimore Ravens. I can foresee myself sacking the Kansas City Chiefs quarterback Patrick Mahomes. I can write down my goal of playing defensive end in the NFL every morning. I can work out every day at the gym, lift weights, and run five miles daily. I can wear a Ravens jersey and tell everyone I meet that I'll be the next defensive end for the Ravens. However, it will still never happen. Obviously, being optimistic and hopeful is not enough. There must be at least an element of realism in the goal fueled by your optimism.

However, having said that, the error that 99 percent of us make is either to never set goals or to make our goals too small. Microsoft was built by a college dropout, Bill Gates. One of the world's greatest physicists, Stephen Hawking, had to battle through quadriplegia. Michael Jordan, the world's greatest basketball player, was told he wasn't good enough to play on his high school varsity basketball team and was relegated to the JV team. All three men knew they had the ability to succeed at the highest level. They didn't settle for mediocrity. Gates could have settled for a job as a software engineer working for someone with a college degree. Hawkins might have decided that it was too difficult to be a physicist as a quadriplegic. He might have taken a job teaching physics to high school kids. Michael Jordan might have quit basketball altogether at age fifteen after being placed on the JV team.

The message: Set the bar as high as you can without making it physically impossible. Then let no obstacle block your path to achieving your objective. Hope and optimism will always be indispensable to your success.

Optimism vs Depression

Actors and celebrities who have successfully battled depression include Gwyneth Paltrow, Dwayne Johnson, Terry Bradshaw, Sheryl Crow, Owen Wilson, and the wife of ex-vice president, Al Gore, Tipper Gore. In addition, J,K. Rowling, author of the Harry Potter series, and Buzz Aldrin who landed on the Moon admit to feeling depressed. There are an estimated 350 million people worldwide who suffer from depression.

Abraham Lincoln, in spite of severe bouts of depression, achieved amazing success as our 16th President, freeing the slaves and winning the civil war. (www.huffpost.com/entry/successful-people-with-de_n_5570970)

Depression is self-hate.

Hating yourself is 180 degrees opposite of God's love for you. Asking God to help you overcome your depression if a first step, of course. Yet, there is more.

10 "This is love: not that we loved God, but that he loved us and sent his son as an atoning sacrifice for our sins." 1 John 4:9-10."

When I was attending law school in San Francisco, I started doubting whether I ever wanted to practice law. At the same time, I had split up with a girlfriend, gained some weight and I had lost all focus of what I wanted to do with my life at age 24. Falling into depression, I began feeling sorry for myself. The food did not taste good. Even my favorite ice cream, rum raisin, was tasteless. I started avoiding people at school. I even stopped attending law school for six weeks. In my job as a law clerk for the Public Defender's office in Oakland, I was showing up late and failing to do the legal research and writing that was required of me. As a poor law student, I also was worrying incessantly how I would afford to pay the rent on my apartment and keep my car running. In my pity party, I felt that everyone at school, work, and my social life was against me.

At the time, I was reading a self-help book which described depression as a person hating themselves.

Eventually, a light turned on in my psyche. I hated myself. Even to this day, I cannot recall the title of that book.

However, the book asked me: With all the problems you're facing, and all the people and circumstances you feel are arrayed against poor little you, what good does it do for you to hate yourself? So, if everyone else and everything else was truly conspiring against me, at the very least, I needed to be cheerleading for myself!

From that day forward, I determined to stop hating myself and be my own best friend.

Even after I emerged from my gloom and realized that not everyone was against me, I have always maintained the attitude of "never hate myself." Always be on my own side. The world is vicious enough.

If you approach depression as I did, you too will find it quite impossible to remain depressed for very long.

When I think of depression, I also recall the Movie, Dick Tracy (1990). Warren Beatty plays Dick Tracy, the detective. Madonna plays the villainous night club singer, "Breathless Mahoney." Dick Tracy (Beatty) is trying to determine if Mahoney is on his side or the bad guy's side. Tracy asks Mahoney (Madonna), "Whose side are you on?" Mahoney (Madonna) replies: "the side I'm always on, my side."

You simply can't be depressed if you are on your own side!

Similarly, if we apply Principle # 5, Optimism, to the problem of depression, the solution emerges quickly. Yet, you will ask me, how do you flip from hating yourself to suddenly looking forward to the future and being hopeful in anticipation of success and happiness. If I recently lost my job, the doctor diagnosed me with cancer, or my spouse walked out, how do I apply optimism to these scenarios?

If your goal is an optimistic attitude, hopeful for future success, then you will need to start thinking optimistic thoughts even though your brain tells you it doesn't feel like it. Now, you object again and tell me that you might be able to do that for an hour, a day or even a week. However, at some point your mind will revert to obsessing over the job you lost, the cancer diagnosis or the husband/wife who left you all alone.

Yet, if we apply Principle #4, Perseverance, again, we find the solution to your fear of being unable to maintain a regimen of optimism. Perseverance is simply the attitude once expressed by Winston Churchill: "Never, Never, ever give up." Perseverance produces success. Consequently, when you are again tempted to think negatively about your life and circumstances, you realize the power of perseverance and self-discipline in order to maintain an attitude of optimism. In order to grow our Perseverance, Principle #16, Self-discipline, will remind us that sometimes we must do what we do not like to do in order to achieve the results we desire. If you are struggling with depression, also refer to Principle #16, Sefl-discipline, to further anchor your foundation for your perseverance and your ultimate victory.

Although this process is easy to describe, you may feel that it is impossible to implement for your life. You tell me that you are not strong enough, smart enough or disciplined enough to follow this regimen. What is the alternative? I'm not a doctor who can prescribe Prozac or Zoloft to mask your depression. I am a psychiatrist or psychologist who you can visit with for extensive counselling sessions.

However, if you do follow these principles, you will not require drugs or the services of professional counselors to cure you of feelings of hopelessness, sadness, and fear.

Optimism vs. Anxiety

What is anxiety? "Anxiety is an emotion characterized by feelings of tension, worried thoughts and physical changes like increased blood pressure." (American Psychological Association, www.apa.org > topics > anxiety.)

What did Jesus say about anxiety?

"Therefore, I tell you, do not be anxious about your life, what you eat or what you will drink, nor about your body, what you will put on. Is life not more than food, and the body more than clothing? Look at the birds of the air: they neither sow nor reap nor gather into barns, and yet your heavenly Father feeds them. Are you not of more value than they? And which of you by being anxious can add a single hour to his span of life? And why are you anxious about clothing?

Consider the lilies of the field, how they grow: they neither toil nor spin, yet I tell you, even Solomon in all his glory was not arrayed like one of these. But, if God so clothes the grass of the field, which today is alive and tomorrow is thrown into the oven, will he not much more clothe you, O you of little faith?" (Matthew, 6: 25-34, NIV)

Be anxious about nothing.

Oprah Winfrey, in a 2013 interview, said that anxiety nearly caused her to have a nervous breakdown.

(Celebrities with Anxiety (webmd.com) If one of the richest women in the world nearly succumbed to her fears and worries, so can you and I, if we don't rely upon the power of our creator.

When I think of anxiety, sweaty palms, shaky hands and one eye twitching come to mind. I recall, at age 16, interviewing for my first summer job at the Baltimore library. I was so afraid that the woman hiring me would see my legs quivering in the chair as she spoke to me about shelving books as a summer page in the downtown Enoch Pratt library. Although there was absolutely nothing for me to be anxious about, fear and dread consumed me for the less than 15-minute interview. The object of our fear does not need to be real for us to create the nightmare of extreme anxiety.

Millions of prescriptions for Xanax and Zoloft testify to the problems Americans suffer today with anxiety. Children with anxiety disorders are often misdiagnosed and given drugs for attention deficit disorders.

If we can only exercise our faith in God instead of relying upon pills in a bottle to calm our every fear,

We can build a culture of bold and courageous men and women. In the New Testament, a father brings is demon possessed son to

Jesus asking for help. After describing how the demon had caused his son to fall into fire or water in order to kill him, the father says to Jesus, "If you can do anything , have compassion on us and help us." Obviously, the man's faith was weak when he uses the words "if you can," when addressing Christ. Jesus responds, "If you believe, all things are possible to him who believes." The father of the boy replies, " Lord I believe, help my unbelief." Mark 9: 17-27. The father was admitting that his faith was weak and simply asked Jesus to make his faith stronger by helping him with his doubts - his "unbelief."

When I am feeling anxious about starting a new book, speaking at a seminar, on the radio, or television, I ask the Lord to help me with my "unbelief." Although I always feel equipped with some degree of faith in both God and my own abilities, I confess to suffering some doubts about the success of the speech, meeting, book, or interview. That is where I ask God to help me with my unbelief. Unfortunately, most of us are often frozen by our anxieties to the point that we're paralyzed from taking action. We translate our nervous voice, our sweaty hands and shaking knees into retreating from the challenge because we think we lack confidence in ourselves and insufficient faith in the Lord. However, Jesus did not require the possessed boy's dad to exhibit perfect faith prior to exorcising the demon from his son. The father merely admitted to the weaknesses in his faith when he requested Christ's intervention.

What are you fearful of doing because your faith in God is insufficient? Ask the Lord to reach out to you where you are and help you with your unbelief. You may have 90% of the faith you think you need or just 1%. Either way, Christ will provide either the extra 10% or the extra 99% to make it happen!

I recall when I was hired as a Special Agent with the F.B.I. With zero experience with firearms and no law enforcement or military training, I was thrust into a paramilitary environment at the F.B.I Academy in Quantico, Virginia. Most of the other new agents were skilled in shooting as a result of army, navy, or police experience. When I started training at the firing range with handguns and rifles, I was fearful that my marksmanship would be sadly lacking compared with my fellow agents who had already developed accuracy on the range. The F.B.I. required that each agent display a proficiency in a timed course of shooting by no later than the 8th week of training. With a .38 caliber revolver with a short snub nose barrel, we were required to hit targets from as far away as 25 and 50 yards. If we failed to qualify by the 8th week, our employment was immediately terminated, and we were sent home. At the conclusion of the 1st 8 weeks, I was still failing to attain the required score to pass on the firing range. However, even though I had failed to "qualify" on all the practice tests prior to the "final exam," I exhibited faith on the morning of that final day on the range. My roommate asked me at breakfast if I "was going to do it." I still recall my response, "No two ways about it. I'm going to make it today." With all the pressure of "win or go home," I asked the Lord to help me with my unbelief that morning.

He did. I qualified.

Boldness is a mighty asset when confronting fear. That is boldness in spite of our fears. In the Old Testament, the Jewish Queen, Esther, displayed unbelievable courage when she appeared in the court of her husband, King Xerxes and asked him to save her people from the slaughter at the hands of . Haman, King Xerxes assistant. Haman had secretly planned the extermination of the Jews in the Persian empire. However, it was a crime punishable by death if Esther were to appear in the King's Court without invitation unless the King held out his golden scepter to her. Esther prayed and asked the Lord to motivate the king to spare her when she made her request. Esther was fearful that the King might have her executed.

However, in the face of her fear, she marched into the court and made her request, first inviting the King to a banquet. Subsequently, at the banquet, the King acceded to her request, saved the Jewish people, and ordered that his assistant, Haman, be hanged. Certainly, God was fully aware of Esther's fears. The Lord knew that in order for Esther to appear before King Xerxes, he must first help her with her unbelief. (Esther Chapter 4 and 5, NKJV)

Most of us have never faced a crisis where the failure of our faith or the lack of our boldness might result in our instant death as Queen Esther did. However, on a daily basis, we often fail to speak up when a friend, co-worker or boss says something that conflicts with our deeply held moral or spiritual beliefs. We fear our friend's or our boss's disapproval, ridicule or even their disgust; I challenge you to speak up the next time your beliefs are denounced, and you are tempted to stay silent. Demand of yourself that you think of Queen Esther and her willingness to risk death to speak truth. If you do, you will most certainly find the courage to disagree and announce your truth. You will probably be surprised when they retreat or cower before your strength and wisdom if indeed your faith is grounded in God's truth. When you finish that conversation, you will walk away with a newfound confidence, fearlessness and perhaps a bit of Hutzpah!

Optimism: Actions for Follow-Up, Week #5

#1: Think about your attitude toward your job, business, health, and family. Resolve to speak only positively in every conversation you have at work, home, and play this week! This will be difficult at first as you catch yourself starting to say negative things about news, the weather, politicians, and somebody else's kids!

#2: Think about your career and where you want to be in one year, five years, and ten years. However, focus on a successful future. What promotion do you aspire to in five years? What do you want your net worth to be in ten years? Where do you see you and your spouse enjoying your retirement?

#3: List the fears you have for the next one, five, and ten years. List each fear with a positive goal/outcome on a piece of paper. This should be the opposite of whatever is scaring you. If you fear going broke, list your anticipated investment in the stock market or real estate and the financial success it will create.

#4: Consider your friends and coworkers. Which of these people is a negative thinker, and who almost always projects a positive attitude? Start spending more time with positive friends and less time with the negative ones.

#5: List the one goal you would love to accomplish that you think is totally out of reach. Resolve to achieve that goal in one, five, or ten years. Begin thinking and reciting all the positive thoughts you would need to have in order to achieve that goal. As an example, perhaps you always wanted to learn how to fly a small plane. Start thinking about how great it would make you feel when you received your pilot's license.

#6: Enumerate on paper all the steps required to achieve the goal of #5. Next to each item, write how you will accomplish that step. Do not allow negative thoughts of how impossible it may be to fulfill each step of your new plan. Stay positive. For example, if you need money to earn a pilot's license, list each step you need to acquire the funds to make that possible.

#7: Pray that the Lord will open your mind to faith and hope as the Bible promises. Constantly, daily, thank the Lord for all the good things in your life. These should include your health, your wealth, your family, and of course the love of God.

Chapter 10
Week #6
Principle: GENOROSITY

Being Generous vs. Being a Stingy Miser

When I was working as a financial advisor, a new client , a software engineer, was referred to me. This man was interested in investing his life savings for retirement and purchasing a franchise for him and his wife to operate. At our first meeting, before we started discussing his financial goals, assets, and retirement plans, he said, "Will you give me a discount today?" I was surprised. As financial advisors and planners, we didn't offer discount coupons. I said no. I advised him of our standard pricing structure based upon the total value of the funds he was investing. After acknowledging that he understood, he asked me again at the end of our meeting to give him a discount. I again advised him of our pricing. He did, however, agree to become a client that day. However, for the next year, every time I called him or met with him, he requested the discount. These repeated requests resulted in my feeling irritated, awkward, and resentful since I had to brace myself prior to each encounter. Consequently, I abbreviated my meetings with him and increased the intervals between meetings. As a result, although not intentional, my service and follow-up for this man were significantly less than for my other clients. The business relationship was damaged by the client's cheapness.

This analogy extends to contract negotiations, taking your assistant to lunch, paying your employees, and taking care of your spouse and children. If you're paying your employee minimum wage while your competitor pays three dollars more per hour, don't expect employee loyalty. If you order your assistant a Big Mac and fries for his or her birthday, you'd better start drafting your job posting for a new employee. If you think you can't afford to take your spouse for a weekend at the coast on your anniversary, can you afford the cost of a divorce lawyer?

Finally, being a miser alienates coworkers, friends, and family. If you go to dinner with your friend, your coworker, or your adult kids, do you usually try to avoid picking up the check? Fewer friends and estranged family members will be the result.

Principle #6: Generosity – Be Generous

2 Corinthians 9:6–8: "Remember this: Whoever sows sparingly will also reap sparingly, and whoever sows generously will also reap generously. Each of you should give what you have decided in your heart to give, not reluctantly or under compulsion, for God loves a cheerful giver."

Outside of the Bible, in the purely secular business book Give and Take (2013), Adam Grant, the author, points out, "Givers are a huge asset to the companies they work for because they make others more effective. They have larger networks that make problem-solving faster and easier. They take the initiative to mentor and train new hires. They pick up the slack when others are overworked. And they foster a sense of loyalty among employees and customers."

What is the upfront cost of being generous?

Obviously, picking up the check after lunch will cost you $40 or $50 out of your wallet. For the priceless asset of a genuine friendship, you're getting away cheap! Of course, if the "friend" expects you to foot the bill every time you meet, you might reconsider whether this person is a friend indeed.

Or should you pay a bonus to an employee who is especially loyal and works very diligently for you?

Consider the cost of losing this employee and trying to replace her. Again, the bonus you pay out is a very cheap way of retaining great people. Besides, your generosity will be a blessing in your own life.

Does Generosity Pay?

Well, the University of Notre Dame says so:

"Is it really more blessed to give than to receive? If you asked the two separate groups of researchers who recently reviewed the psychological literature on generosity, their answer would be a resounding "Yes." After analyzing hundreds of studies, both teams found that the motivation to help others comes with an impressive list of benefits. People who are "otherish" rather than selfish tend to live longer, for example. And they also experience higher levels of wellbeing, greater self-esteem, more positive emotions, and stronger relationships." (Notre Dame Deloitte Center for Ethical Leadership, 2022, ethicalleadership.nd.edu)

A new study adds one even more surprising detail to our picture of generosity. A team of researchers led by Kimmo Erikson combed through data from the United States, the UK, and twenty-three other European Countries and found that generous people have healthier bodies, minds, and relationships—and in the long run, they actually make more money than people who are selfish (Kimmo Eriksson Generosity Pays: Selfish People Have Fewer Children and Earn Less Money," Journal of Personality, October 17, 2018)

In other words, it literally pays to be generous!

In December, I received free in the mail six beautiful Christmas cards in a large, flowery envelope from a national Christian charity that I had never given any money to. After reading over their plea for financial help and considering the cost to them of these baby

Jesus in the manger cards, I sent them a donation. Obviously, the generosity of the Christian charity paid a nice dividend for them!

A number of years ago, when I first started my practice as a financial advisor, I taught a financial planning seminar at a large retirement home near Portland, Oregon. Two elderly ladies approached me after the program and asked if I would meet with them to discuss providing an investment program for them. After meeting with them at their apartment, I opened an account for each of them. The older lady had amassed a large amount of savings as a result of an inheritance from her father. The slightly younger woman, Susan (not her real name), about seventy-five years old, had taught high school English for many years and had managed to save a relatively small amount of money in the bank. They both requested that I meet with them regularly at the retirement home to review their accounts and have lunch. After about a year, the older woman passed away. The retired schoolteacher then moved away to Eugene, Oregon, which then became a two-hour drive from my office for each meeting. Still, Susan asked me to meet with her and have lunch with her on a regular basis. At this point, with her small investment account, it was not worth my time to drive over two hours, have lunch with her and call her in between meetings just to say hello.

However, I started calling her in between meetings just to make sure she was OK. Yet Susan was always glad to hear from me and excited about our lunch meetings .Susan was all alone, had no children, and had never married. Her closest friends lived in Arizona, about a thousand miles away. I personally felt that I was her only friend in the state of Oregon, and the Lord would certainly want me to be generous with my time. So, I continued to meet with her at the same pancake house.

About eighteen months after her friend died, Susan also passed away. Sometime later, I was notified by her executor that she had left me $25,000 in her will. Certainly, I had never expected to be compensated for reaching out in friendship to another human being who was very lonely.

Obviously, we should not be reaching out to lonely people with the ulterior motive of being financially compensated in return. However, the product of generosity is a blessing. On the other hand, stinginess will seldom be rewarded. Whether the blessing is financial, spiritual, or a new friendship, you will never regret giving of your time or money, or just giving someone a compliment. Depression, anxiety, and worry plague our culture like never before. Think about boosting someone else's morale today.

In the Old Testament (1 Kings 17:10–16), we find amazing generosity by the widow of Zarephath. During a famine, the widow was going to use her very last bit of flour to bake bread for her and her son. She even tells the prophet of God Elijah, that after she eats it, she and her son will have no more food and they will die. Nevertheless, Elijah, displaying what appears as hutzpah, asks her to bake him some bread! The widow agrees and bakes him bread from her last bit of flour. Yet Elijah then promises her that her jar of flour will never run out again. Later, her son dies, Elijah prays, and her son is resurrected from the dead. For the Widow's generosity, she received a guarantee of food for life and the restoration of her son's life! That's a pretty good return on investment for the widow!

Generosity: Actions for Follow-Up, Week #6

#1: Whom can you help today financially? This can be a person who is homeless, a family member, or a coworker or friend who may just need you to take them to lunch.

#2: Whom can you help today by being generous with your time? You can help a coworker with a project. Assist your child with their homework; assist your spouse at home.

#3: What charity can you contribute to? As a Christian, perhaps give more to your local church or another ministry. Of course, for a non-Christian, there are literally thousands of secular charities such as United Way.

#4: Whom can you visit in the hospital or at least write a get-well card to if none of your friends or family are hospitalized? In my former business as a financial advisor, I made a practice of calling, praying with, and sending a card to any client who was ill. Be sure to write a personal note when you send the card and follow up with an immediate phone call.

#5: Look ahead and plan how you can make a steady contribution to a charity and/or a person in need of help.

#6: Longer term, how can you generously donate your time to help another person(s)?

#7: Ask the Lord how you can be more generous with your time and money. As a nonbeliever, meditate upon those who need your assistance and how you might help them.

Chapter 11
Week #7
Principle: HARD WORK

Hard Work vs. TGIF and Doing the Minimum to Get By

An article headline by Travis Bradberry says, "Gallup research shows that 70% of employees consider themselves to be disengaged at work" (World Economic Forum, November 4, 2016). If you're disengaged at work, you obviously lack the ability to set new goals and the persistence to chase after their achievement.

Indeed, if 70 percent of your coworkers are disengaged, you are blessed with an amazing opportunity to be promoted! If you are ambitious, you need to compete with only 30 percent of the employees around you for a better job!

However, some of this apparent employee apathy may be due to our government's tax and benefit policies. Employees are often discouraged from seeking higher-paying jobs due to taxes.

Progressive federal, state, and local taxes, in addition to Social Security withholding, sharply reduce the net paycheck to the point that some workers may feel there are insufficient incentives to undertake additional responsibilities, duties, and stress.

There are other benefits to doing the minimum to get by without getting fired. You don't put in the extra hours; you have more free time. At first blush, it would appear that your stress level would be lower. However, if you're perceived as indifferent and lazy by your employer, it is probable that your boss will not value your contribution. Consequently, you will be the prime candidate to be assigned the most mundane and stressful tasks. In addition, if layoffs occur, you will be first in line to lose your job. Your coworkers may not want to associate with someone who isn't interested in their job and their company. You will forfeit the opportunity for promotion and pay raises. Consequently, you may not be able to afford to purchase a home or a new car or to take a nice vacation. Those extra hours at home may not be the opportunity to relax and enjoy the life that you had envisioned.

Principle #7: Hard Work, Your Work Ethic

"Whatever you do, work heartily, as for the Lord and not for men, knowing that from the Lord you will receive the inheritance as your reward. You are serving the Lord Christ." (Colossians 3:23–24).

For Christians, here is the motivation for your hard work: Whatever you do, you are doing it for God. You are His child and His servant.

"Commit your work to the Lord, and your plans will be established." (Proverbs 16:3, ESV).

"You shall eat the fruit of the labor of your hands; you shall be blessed, and it shall be well with you" (Psalms 128:2, KJV).

Here, God is promising to reward our hard work with the "establishment of our plans" and, even more importantly, His "blessing" and that it "shall be well with you."

Even if you're not a believer, by working hard, "you shall be blessed." We often refer to this concept as the Puritan work ethic. The establishment of a free enterprise, capitalistic economy in America is testimony to the success of this work ethic. In America, we grew a meritocracy based upon hard work. Since the nineteenth century, American entrepreneurs have built their own businesses into multimillion-dollar corporations at the highest levels. However, you don't need to be a risk-taking entrepreneur to create a middle-class lifestyle and a net worth of over a million dollars. You can work in middle management for the government or private sector, save your money, and easily retire with a million dollars or more today. Blue-collar workers toiling on the assembly line at General Motors can easily pass the million-dollar bar with regular savings in their 401k or company retirement plan. The key is steadfastness in your job, hard work, and persistence in savings and investment.

Hard Work: Actions for Follow-Up, Week #7

#1: Examine your past. When have you worked hard in a job and reaped the rewards of success? It may have been a minimum-wage job as a waitress. The rewards may have been a fifty-cent-an-hour raise or a "good job, well done" from your boss. When have you given less than your best, resulting in missing out on a promotion, getting a dead-end assignment, or even losing your job?

#2: Determine which of your job duties are of paramount importance to your employer. If you own the business, what areas of your work will produce the greatest return on investment by focusing more effort there? List those important job duties or areas of focus for your business that will benefit most from your new work commitment. Examine your workday. Be honest with yourself. If you already are giving 100 percent to your job or business, then skip the remaining steps and move on. Congratulations on your fantastic work ethic!

#3: What obstacles will you encounter by increasing your workload in the job duties and business areas you selected? For example, if you plan to spend more of your time generating new sales, are you going to spend less time doing the administrative tasks that are part of your responsibilities? If that is your intention, then you are wasting your time. Do not exchange success in one sphere for failure in another. List these obstacles and specify how you will overcome them.

#4: What sacrifices will you need to make in order to work harder to achieve your career goals? For example, if you need to work a nine-hour day instead of an eight-hour day to achieve a career objective, will you need to sacrifice your time playing video games, watching television, or taking a long lunch?

#5: If you decline to work harder in your job now, what will the future look like? Will you be passed over for promotion? Will your income stagnate? Will you forfeit an opportunity for retirement or settle for less income when you do retire?

#6: Now focus all your enthusiasm and effort on working harder in those capacities. Dedicate yourself on a daily basis to the new regimen at work. Wake up thirty minutes earlier. Stay at your office thirty minutes longer. Watch the extra effort pay off in your career and your paycheck!

#7: Pray that the Lord leads you in the establishment of this new work regimen without sacrificing relations with family and friends. However, also ask the Lord to help you forgive yourself when you occasionally waste time, oversleep, or are late for work. Remember to always be your own best friend and to treat yourself with compassion as well.

Chapter 12
Week #8
Principle: OBEDIENCE

Being Obedient vs. Being Disobedient and Breaking the Rules

We have all heard that the rules that apply to us don't apply to the rich and famous.

"If you believe that you're just more deserving than others, you're probably not too fond of following instructions. People with a greater sense of entitlement are less likely to follow instructions than less entitled people, according to new research published in Social Psychological and Personality Science. It seemed like entitled people weren't following instructions because they believed the instructions were an unfair imposition on them. Future research should examine how to get entitled individuals to follow instructions" (Eric W. Dolan, "It's Hard to Get Entitled People to Follow Instructions, Study Finds," PsyPs, January 29, 2018).

There is an intersection between the character qualities of obedience and humility. We can conclude from the study that the humbler you are, the more likely you are to obey the rules. The haughty and arrogant person may display a reckless disregard for those rules. Isn't this lack of humility proven by recent history? Hitler and Stalin were proud, arrogant men with no regard for the borders of other nations or the lives of the people who lived there. Indeed, lack of humility and breaking the rules are almost indigenous to the character of dictators and arrogant business leaders as well. Bernie Madoff exemplifies that haughty disregard for the rules. Madoff, of course, defrauded investors and was sent to prison.

Our hip culture promotes excesses in personal use of drugs, alcohol, casual sex, and pornography. These behaviors once represented disobedience to societal rules and norms. Today, at worst, you may suffer a very light penalty for these behaviors. However, obedience to biblical morality demands the absolute avoidance of illegal drugs and the consumption of excessive alcohol. Obedience to biblical truth requires abstaining from premarital sex, pornography, and same-sex marriage.

Yet, according to both our hip and corporate cultures, righteous obedience means conformity to concepts of political correctness. Celebration of all forms of gay or bisexual behavior is imperative to your acceptance by secular culture. Adherence to theories of "climate change," "social justice," and "critical race theory" is paramount. However, it is impossible to find a biblical anchor for these beliefs. When confronted with these ideas, you should simply follow the golden rule: "In everything, do unto others as you would have them do to you." (Matthew 7:12).

Principle #8: Be Obedient

"Have confidence in your leaders and submit to their authority, because they keep watch over you as those who must give an account. Do this so that their work will be a joy, not a burden, for that would be of no benefit to you" (Hebrews 13:17).

Insubordination to your supervisor's direct orders is, of course, a way to not get promoted. It's a quick means of getting fired.

Obedience, however, encompasses much more than just a willingness to follow orders. Being chronically late for work, being late to complete assignments, and goofing off at work are all forms of disobedience on the job. Each in its own right will result in career stagnation at best or simply losing your job.

Being disrespectful to your boss and calling in sick when you're going to the beach also fall under the category of disobedience. Sexually harassing a coworker is certainly will always be contrary to company policy and constitutes insubordination.

Even if you don't believe in an Almighty God, you will want to eliminate even the possibility of any of these behaviors if you expect to achieve career and financial success.

There, however, is a noteworthy exception to this rule. If your employer is asking you to take actions that are illegal, unethical, or contrary to your deeply held religious beliefs, you should not feel any compunction about saying no. Immediately, you should report the supervisor to your senior management personnel. If your company is imposing a new policy that you believe to be illegal, unethical, or contrary to your religious beliefs, you may need to contact the local district attorney's office and report your employer. If that is not feasible, you may need to hire a private lawyer, the American Center for Law and Justice, or Alliance Defending Freedom.

However, in the main, following instructions in the workplace will single you out as a person who can be trusted by the organization to get things done.

Being Obedient: Actions for Follow-Up, Week #8

#1: When in the past have you been obedient to authority in your career, and it has paid off for you? For example, if you have been promoted, it's likely that your record of obedience to your supervisor(s) caused them to be confident you would be successful in a new position. When were you disobedient? Do you think your disobedience might have caused you to miss out on a promotion or other job benefit? For example, if you were habitually late for work or were often sarcastic in responding to supervisors, might that have jeopardized your opportunities for advancement?

#2: Determine what areas of obedience you will need to improve to reach your career goals. Make a list of them on paper and review it.

#3: What obstacles might prevent you from becoming a more obedient employee? If you own a business, your issues regarding obedience may relate more to how you treat your employees and whether your business is obedient to all federal, state, and local laws and regulations. For example, as a business owner, are your tax returns in full compliance with the law? The obstacle may be that you will need to pay more taxes, as difficult as that may be. For the employee who is often late to work, the obstacle may be going to bed too late at night, not getting enough sleep, and waking up too late.

#4: What sacrifices will you need to make to be more obedient in the future? Obedience itself is a sacrifice. It is the sacrifice of doing what your employer wants instead of what you want to do. For the businessperson, it is the sacrifice of doing what the government may require your company to do instead of what you want your company to do.

#5: If you continue in your disobedience in the area of _____, what will your future look like in one year, five years, and ten years? For example, as an employee, if you don't complete your job in the time allotted on a repetitive basis, what is the likelihood that you will ever be promoted? If your business is constantly violating government regulations, will your company eventually be shut down or penalized? How can you grow a business or career when you're not in compliance?

#6: Today, think about all the areas of your life where you have not been obedient to your employer, your family, and the Lord. Resolve today to be obedient in those areas each day, regardless of the sacrifice you will be required to make. Meditate upon these areas and make the same resolution.

#7: As a Christian, ask God to assist you in being obedient to him at work and at home. You might also request a trusted friend to mentor you. For example, have that mentor ask you once a week if you truly have been obedient in the areas you are working on so that you may be kept accountable.

Chapter 13
Week #9
Principle: LOYALTY

Being Loyal vs. Being Disloyal and Unreliable

Insurance companies spend billions of dollars trying to establish brand loyalty for a very necessary consumer purchase, auto insurance. I see ads from Liberty Mutual, State Farm, Farmers, Allstate, and Progressive, among others, constantly promoting their insurance in flashy commercials on television. Yet consulting firm Smart Insights shows that when considering car insurance renewals, 86 percent of consumers do research online before making the purchase. These interactions take place across tablets, PCs, and smartphones (Blaise Lucey, "Customer Experience in the Age of Disloyalty," MarTech Performance Marketing, June 23, 2016). Obviously, consumers aren't showing brand loyalty to the insurance companies. Perhaps, if the insurers spent more money assisting their customers, they wouldn't need to spend as much on television commercials.

Fifty years ago, it was traditional to work for the same company for thirty or forty years and retire with a pension and a gold watch. Today, loyalty to an employer, a business, and a spouse is viewed as passé. Conversely, employers are less loyal to workers than ever before. Since the 1980s, many CEOs have shown no compassion or loyalty to employees. When revenues and profits decline, companies are quick to axe their payrolls, leaving their workers in unemployment lines. Both employer and employee view each other as untrustworthy and unreliable.

In business, contracts are breached, litigation ensues, and often the only winners are the lawyers. The millennial generation, more than any other, wants to work to live, not live to work. Consequently, both employee and employer are often the casualties of this new attitude.

As a result, as either an employer or a worker, today you have a unique opportunity to stand out in a transient corporate culture.

Principle #9: Loyalty – Be Loyal

It is significant that the Old Testament of the Bible speaks of the loyalty of an exiled general to King David at a time when the king was under attack: "But Ittai answered the king, 'As the Lord lives, and as my lord the king lives, wherever my lord the king shall be, whether for death or for life, there also will your servant be.'" (2 Samuel 15:21). Ittai, an exiled foreigner, pledged his loyalty to King David, who was besieged by his son, Absalom, at the time.

"When confronted with a challenge, the committed heart will search for a solution. The undecided heart searches for an escape."—Andy Andrews, The Traveler's Gift, 2002, Thomas Nelson Publishing.

If you are truly committed to your job, your business, and your family, you will stay on the project or the job until you solve the problem. That is every employer's hope and expectation for their workers. If you, the employee, are undecided about your commitment, you are likely to walk away at the first sign of a roadblock to your success. Obviously, the same analysis applies to the businessperson who is not committed to his or her business.

"Employee loyalty begins with employer loyalty. Your employees should know that if they do the job they were hired to do with a reasonable amount of competence and efficiency, you will support them."—Harvey Mackay, (www.brainyquote.com)

If you are the employer, your commitment to loyalty to your employee is paramount if you expect the same from that employee. A study led by Stanford Graduate School of Business professor Jeffrey Pfeffer revealed that companies are no longer favoring their loyal, hardworking employees as they used to." (Batuhan BalciL, "Research Shows Employees Are Not Rewarded for Their Loyalty," Stanford Daily, March 2, 2015). In our age of employee grievances, litigation, and unionism, employers are foolish to fail to reward employees with bonuses, time off, and opportunities for education, job growth, and promotion.

I was listening to a sports talk show recently where the host was harshly criticizing a college football coach because he quit coaching at a major university to take a million-dollar pay raise to coach at another school. The host chastised the coach for lacking any loyalty to his former school. Not more than five minutes later, the same host congratulated another major university for firing its head coach for not having a winning record after only a single season. Loyalty goes both ways!

If you develop a reputation for moving from one job to another simply to grab a bigger paycheck somewhere else, employers will view you as "unstable" and be very reluctant to employ you. If you own a business and expect "brand loyalty," you need to place your customers' satisfaction as your number one priority. Consumers appreciate a company that overwhelms them with service, not ads.

For years, Nordstrom has been able to charge higher prices than other retailers because its customers have viewed the company as loyal to them. One of the primary ways Nordstrom has distinguished itself from the competition is their lifetime guarantee policy. This legendary return policy is best exemplified by the (perhaps mythic) tire story:

A man walks into the Anchorage, Alaska, Nordstrom store and wants to return a set of tires despite the fact that Nordstrom doesn't sell tires. The store that previously occupied the same space did, though, and the Nordstrom manager still decides to refund the customer his money—for a product they didn't even sell! (What We Can All Learn from Nordstrom's Exceptional Success > (predictableprofits.com P. 38)

Now, that's loyalty!

Loyalty: Actions for Follow-Up, Week #9

#1: When has loyalty to your employer or to customers paid off for you in the past? When I was working as a financial advisor/stockbroker, a very elderly client of mine told me she was going to a car dealer to buy a Buick. Since I'm aware that elderly people are sometimes taken advantage of by fast-talking salesmen, I offered to accompany her to the dealership in Portland, Oregon. Fortunately, I was able to assist her in purchasing her new car at a very reasonable price. Later, I received calls from her family thanking me for helping their mom buy the car. Subsequently, those family members became outstanding and loyal clients.

#2 When have you regretted not being loyal to your company, your customers, or your family?

#3: Examine your personal history of loyalty to your company, your customers, and your family. List the areas in which you need to improve.

#4: What obstacles might prevent you from being a more loyal employee, business owner, or spouse? Loyalty to an employee who has been with you for a long time might require that you retain him or her even though he or she may be less productive after many years of service. The obstacle may be your desire to maximize profits. The Lord will certainly bless you for your loyalty to your employees.

For example, if you are an auto mechanic at a local shop and you start inviting some of the shop's loyal customers to secretly have their repairs done at your house during your off hours for 20% cheaper, you are stealing business from your employer.

As for your spouse, if you are disloyal, you are harming yourself and your relationship. Obviously, it will be more difficult to focus on your job or business if you're going through a divorce or relationship breakup.

#5: What sacrifices will you need to make to remain loyal? As the employee, you may sacrifice extra income now by turning down an offer from another employer to pay you a little more money. Of course, if you remain loyal, you may receive an opportunity for a promotion and higher pay where you are. Also, in exchange for the new employer's offer of a higher salary, working conditions may be less desirable, and there might not be an opportunity for advancement. Showing old-fashioned loyalty to others often pays off in the long run.

As a business owner, when you spend more on customer service—e.g., allowing a liberal return policy, guaranteeing the performance of your products or services—you will incur added expenses. Will you accept these short-term sacrifices in order to attract more customers and more long-term revenue?

#6: If you persist in disloyalty to your company, your customers, or your spouse, what will your life look like in one year, five years, and ten years? Write this out. For example, disloyal employees are usually terminated. Companies that fail to look out for their customers often go bankrupt. If you are cheating on your spouse, you may become divorced and very lonely.

#7: Launch your loyalty regimen! Step it up with your boss, your business, and your husband or wife today. What action can you take today to show your loyalty at home and at work? If you have committed adultery against your spouse, repent of that disloyalty and resolve to be loyal and faithful.

#8: Ask God to help you strive to be loyal at work and at home.

"Dear friend, you are faithful in what you do for the brothers and sisters, even though they are strangers to you." (3 John 1:5 NIV).

Chapter 14
Week #10
Principle: HUMILITY

Being Humble vs. Being Prideful and Arrogant

There is absolutely nothing wrong with being proud of our accomplishments. In fact, you should always take pride in your work. If you're scrubbing the floor or making a sales presentation to the CEO of a Fortune 500 company, display confidence and take pride in every detail of your labors. However, today, it has become commonplace that actors, athletes, and politicians are applauded for their self-conceit and hubris.

The cultural trend toward exalting oneself began in the 1960s with the heavyweight boxing champion Muhammad Ali, constantly declaring himself to be "the greatest." As a result, the national media anointed Ali as "the greatest." Perhaps he was the greatest boxer ever. However, his Hutzpa in making that declaration caught on with the public. Today, many athletes in basketball, football, baseball, and others have followed suit.

Principle #10: Be Humble

In the Old Testament, the book of Proverbs issues a warning to the person who is arrogant: "Pride goes before destruction, a haughty spirit before a fall. Better to live humbly with the poor than to share plunder with the proud." (Proverbs 16:18–19, ESV). This means that if you are acting prideful, watch out! You are about to fall.

In February 2022, the Russian dictator Vladimir Putin invaded the sovereign democratic nation of Ukraine without provocation.

Putin had been the leader of Russia for over twenty years at the time. Russia possesses the largest nuclear arsenal and one of the most powerful armies in the world. However, upon news of the invasion, the destruction of Ukrainian cities, and the slaughter of innocent civilians, Putin instantly became a pariah in the eyes of most of the world, including his own nation.

In America, we have seen highly respected pastors such as Jimmy Swaggart and televangelist Jim Bakker brought down by scandals created by their own acts of immorality.

Back in the 1970s, our President Richard Nixon opened the door to China, successfully negotiated nuclear arms treaties with the Soviet Union, and founded the Environmental Protection Agency. Yet his legacy was destroyed, and he barely avoided criminal prosecution after participating in a cover-up of the Watergate burglary. Nixon was forced to resign in disgrace. The arrogance of power breeds a false sense of invincibility.

In professional sports, Lance Armstrong, O. J. Simpson, and Tanya Harding fell from the heights of cycling, football, and figure skating to dishonor because they apparently felt they were above the law, exempt from the rules that the rest of us play by.

There is a myriad of other political, religious, sports, and other celebrities who have fallen from grace due to their own puffed-up images of themselves, seeing themselves as above secular and/or moral authority.

Again, Proverbs announces, "The reward of humility and the fear of the Lord are riches, honor, and life." (Proverbs 22:4, New American Standard Bible).

God promises in His word that there is a reward for humility. Riches, honor, and life sound like a pretty good deal to me! Even if you're a nonbeliever, the Bible's cautionary words, coupled with real-life examples we read about each day in the news, should deter you from becoming a braggart.

Yet in our culture today, athletes are often known for their egocentricity. The great basketball player LeBron James basks in the media-made glory of being called "King James." When an NFL player scores a touchdown now, it has become routine for him to do a self-congratulatory dance in the end zone. Way back in 1969, perhaps this trend started when the New York Jets quarterback Joe Namath guaranteed victory over the Baltimore Colts in the Super Bowl. After the Jets win, Namath was lauded with praise for the "confidence" he displayed in making the "guarantee."

However, God may humble you if you display arrogance. In the Old Testament, we see King Nebuchadnezzar humbled by God. The king had a statue of himself constructed. He ordered the people to worship him as God:

As the king was walking on the roof of the royal palace of Babylon, he said, "Is not this the great Babylon I have built as the royal residence, by my mighty power and for the glory of my majesty?"

The words were still on his lips when a voice came from heaven, "This is what is decreed for you, King Nebuchadnezzar: Your royal authority has been taken from you. You will be driven away from people and will live with the wild animals; you will eat grass like cattle. Seven times will pass by for you until you acknowledge that the Most High is sovereign over the kingdoms of men and gives them to anyone he wishes."

Immediately, what had been said about Nebuchadnezzar was fulfilled. He was driven away from people and ate grass like cattle. His body was drenched with the dew of heaven until his hair grew like the feathers of an eagle and his nails like the claws of a bird. (Daniel 4:28–33).

Instead, unlike King Nebuchadnezzar, God expects us to "play" the game of life with confidence in his power to give us success. For the Lord has given us the tools for a victorious life. God may gift you with athletic talent, leadership ability, or aptitude in mathematics or science. As a result of his arrogance, King Nebuchadnezzar "ate grass like cattle" and lived like a "wild animal" for seven years until the Lord finally restored his mind and allowed him to return to his throne again.

Finally, Stephen Tulloch, linebacker for the NFL's Detroit Lions, in a game against the Green Bay Packers on September 24, 2014, sacked Packers quarterback Aaron Rodgers. After the play was over, Tulloch danced on the field, celebrating his takedown of Rogers. In the middle of his dance, he suddenly fell to the ground, clutching his leg. Unfortunately, Tulloch, so proud of doing what he was paid to do, had torn his ACL. He was devastated upon finding that he was sidelined with the injury for the rest of the season! Truly, pride came before his fall! (www.cbssports.com >NFL>news>Stephen-Tulloch).

Yet God does not call us to be without confidence in what we do. A self-confident person is indeed humble. "So do not throw away your confidence; it will be richly rewarded" (Hebrews 10:35–36, New International Version). Here, God is telling us to remain "confident" in order that we receive a "reward."

Being humble is a sign of self-confidence.

Humility: Actions for Follow-Up, Week #10

#1: When have you behaved with humility and yet remained confident? Did you reap a favorable result? When have you acted arrogantly and pridefully? What was the result?

#2: Evaluate your own history. What areas of humility do you need to improve on? At work? In your business? With your family? Most of us are tempted to act with hubris right after we have achieved a major success in our job, business, or personal life. For example, men have often engaged in extramarital affairs shortly after a major business or athletic success. We are often puffed up from the praise of our coworkers, our boss, or our business associates. It is then that we fall prey to misconduct with money, sex, or misuse of authority. List the areas for your improvement. (If you can't find any, that's not something to be proud of!)

#3: What obstacles will you encounter when you proceed to curb your pride and act humbly? For example, in the future, how will you respond to the fawning adulation of a business associate or coworker for simply a job well done?

#4: What sacrifices will you be required to make in order to adopt a humbler demeanor? At work? At home with your spouse and children? For example, do you fear that friends or family will like you less if you're not extolling your own virtues? (In fact, your humility will attract more friends!)

#5: Envision yourself in one, five, and ten years. If you don't temper your pride, how might that affect your life? With your hubris, are you setting yourself up for a fall in the future?

#6: Implement and embrace your new humble lifestyle! Remain confident that you can do all things through Christ. Don't let your self-confidence turn to arrogance. Today, your family and friends should start seeing a difference in your demeanor. Within ninety days, you will be hearing from them about a very positive change they see in you.

#7: Ask God to guide you in your outlook. Don't be afraid of appearing tepid or quiet. God will make certain that your efforts are recognized by others. Take comfort in the lessons of Proverbs. Your very acts of humility shall reflect positively upon you in your business and family life. Remember, Benjamin Franklin added humility to his list of personal character traits he worked on every day.

Chapter 15
Week #11
Principle: FORGIVENESS

Forgiveness vs. Holding a Grudge and Getting Revenge

"Holding onto anger is like drinking poison and expecting the other person to die. In business, forgiveness allows you to cut away the mental clutter, self-doubt, or resentment and focus on the activities and relationships that will help you produce and prosper." (Celeste Giordano, "Why Holding Grudges Is Poison for Your Business," LinkedIn, July 14, 2016).

Recently, a Georgia man was arrested for assault after being denied a straw in a local McDonald's restaurant. After the worker told him she didn't have a straw for his drink, he jumped the counter and beat her. The customer displayed a total lack of patience, tolerance, and forgiveness towards a McDonald's worker who was simply trying to help him. (www.cnn.com/2019/01/02/us/customer-attacks-mcdonalds-employee).

Sixty-nine percent of Americans hold grudges, a new study finds. Not getting a desired job, getting dumped by a boyfriend/girlfriend, or a bad customer experience results in people harboring a grudge. Sixty-three percent of the respondents to a survey noted that they have held grudges against businesses for poor customer service. Significantly, the respondents advised that they were more likely to hold grudges against businesses than against people. In the same study, 53 percent of participants admitted they were too quick to hold a grudge against someone (Bryan Robinson, "New Study Shows the Mental and Physical Harm of Holding Workplace Grudges," Forbes, February 5, 2022).

As much as this research reveals the prevalence and futility of holding grudges, it should be a wake-up call to retail stores and online websites serving consumers. As a result of my personal experience with a homeowner's insurance policy a few years ago, I harbored a grudge against the company for several weeks. Our poolroom walls had been severely damaged as a result of winter storms. Our insurance company sent an adjuster, who determined that the damage was covered by the policy. He assessed the financial damage from the storms to be over $21,000. The adjuster forwarded the $21,000 claim to the Seattle office with his recommendation that it be paid immediately. However, the insurance company denied our claim and advised us that they would pay nothing. My wife and I were told that the damage was due to "dry rot," which was not covered under our policy. Of course, this assessment was made without any evidence and directly contradicted the findings of their adjuster who came to our home. After I expressed my outrage to the Seattle manager, my claim was promptly transferred to a manager in Indiana. The Indiana manager denied our claim again for the same reason and transferred the claim to Houston, Texas. Again, the Texas manager told us the damage was not insurable despite their own adjuster's report. When I protested again, he routed our claim to a regional manager in Los Angeles. This time, four months after the adjuster's report, the company simply paid our claim. There was no explanation or apology. Over the next six months, I related this story to friends, family, and anybody who would listen.

However, what was the consequence of all my criticism of this insurance company? Certainly, I derived no benefit from my venting. The insurance company may have lost a few business opportunities as a result of my diatribe. I spent a lot of time thinking about the unfair treatment I had received. This was the time I could have more usefully spent enjoying my family, reading a good book, or working out. The insurance company did not change its policies as a result of my protests. Finally, after a few months, I decided to forgive those managers and their company. I simply realized that, like myself, they were people who made mistakes in their work. We are not perfect people. Like everyone else, I haven't always done the right thing. I need that forgiveness too.

Since the 1980s, personal customer service has been deemphasized by corporate America. When I called a realtor to find out more information about a house I viewed online, I listened to a recording asking me if I need a mortgage, how much of a down payment I will make, and if I'm an investor or simply looking for a house to live in. After answering the recording's questions, I'm told to expect a 20-to-30-minute hold time. If I'm unable to hold, then someone will call me back. When I ask for a call back, I then am asked by the same recording if I want to sell my own house and the approximate value of my home, and how much I still owe it. Frustrated, I hung up. I try to think about how busy and stressed the person who set up this recording must be, so I can try to forgive them. However, someone less patient than I just might go postal! Forgiveness is really not valued in America today.

Principle #11: Forgive Others

"For if you forgive men their sins, your heavenly Father will also forgive you. But if you do not forgive others their sins, your father will not forgive your sins." (Matthew 6:14–15, NIV).

In the Old Testament book of Genesis, Joseph's brothers are jealous of their father Jacob's favoritism toward Joseph. As a result, they throw him into a cistern and later sell him to an Ishmaelite caravan as a slave. Years later, without food, they come to Egypt and beg Joseph, now an Egyptian official, for food. Joseph, instead of holding a grudge and punishing them for making him a slave, forgives his brothers and provides food to them (Genesis, 50:15, 45:1–15 NIV).

As Christians, we are forgiven for our misdeeds at the cross of Christ. However, in our everyday life, if we are holding a grudge against someone for what we believe they wrongly did to us, Christ is unable to forgive us. Even as a non-Christian, medical science provides evidence of the damage we may be doing to our physical body by harboring an attitude of unforgiveness and anger toward another person.

"Studies have found that the act of forgiveness can reap huge rewards for your health, lowering the risk of heart attack; improving cholesterol levels and sleep; and reducing pain, blood pressure, and levels of anxiety, depression, and stress. And research points to an increase in the forgiveness–health connection as you age." On the other hand, "chronic anger puts you into a fight-or-flight mode, which results in numerous changes in heart rate, blood pressure and immune response. Those changes, then, increase the risk of depression, heart disease and diabetes, among other conditions ("Forgiveness: Your Health Depends Upon It," www.hopkinsmedicine.org/health/wellness-and-prevention/forgiveness-your-health-depends-on-it).

As it relates to work and business, "in one study involving more than 200 employees from both office and manufacturing jobs, forgiveness was 'linked to increased productivity, decreased absenteeism (fewer days missing work), and fewer mental and physical health problems, such as sadness and headaches… Forgiveness also extends outwardly to impact others not involved in the conflict. When colleagues observe others practicing forgiveness, research says it often 'fosters positive emotions that can improve decision-making, cognitive functioning, and the quality of relationships' (Inc. magazine, Marcel Schwantes, "How Practicing Forgiveness Actually Boosts Your Productivity (and Health)," December 14, 2016).

Forgiveness, then, is not just the kind, Christian thing to do; it's good business. You'll be healthier, and you'll make more money!

Forgiveness: Actions for Follow-Up, Week #11

#1: When have you forgiven someone and been blessed by it? Did you feel at peace after forgiving that person? When have you held a grudge? How did that make you feel? How much time did you spend being angry with that person?

#2: Whom do you need to forgive right now? If you have not forgiven someone for an offense against you, why not? Is it really worth jeopardizing your health? Your job? Your business productivity?

#3: What obstacles do you envision preventing you from forgiving another person? Do you think you would be letting them off too easily by forgiving their misconduct toward you? Do you think they might view you as a weak person if you forgive them?

#4: What sacrifices will you need to make in order to forgive that person? Do you feel that if you forgive them, they'll never realize how much they hurt you? Is giving up your anger at them a sacrifice you need to make now?

#5: If you look back one year, five years, and ten years from now, how will you feel if you are still holding a grudge against that person? Still angry? A little bit foolish? That person has moved on with their life and probably forgotten about you, as well as the incident you're still upset about.

#6: Today is the day to forgive those who hurt you! Do it now! Feel blessed and 100 percent healthier in body, mind, and soul. Write down the names of the people you are forgiving and what you're forgiving them for. Then rip up the paper and throw it away.

#7: Ask the Lord to help you retain the forgiving spirit toward that person(s) for the rest of your life. Meditate upon how much better and stronger you feel once you let go of a personal grudge.

Chapter 16
Week #12
Principle: KINDNESS

Being Kind vs. Being Inconsiderate and Ruthless

We often assume that in business, the most cutthroat and ruthless corporate leaders and managers are the most successful. Flattering the boss, demeaning your coworkers, and acting with a sense of superiority and arrogance should pave the way to the executive suite. The perception is that the successful boss should display a sense of dominance, a lack of compassion, and the ability to manipulate both his subordinates and senior management. However, a recent study reveals just the opposite. The research project evaluated the behaviors of one hundred hedge fund investment managers in terms of unselfishness vs. selfishness. They also evaluated narcissistic interactions with coworkers and subordinates. They measured the investment success of the managers evincing the most inconsiderate, ruthless behavior against those whose behavior was not selfish or narcissistic. The researchers found that the managers displaying the selfish behaviors substantially underperformed managers whose behavior was more unselfish and considerate (Leanne Ten Brinke et al., "Hedge Fund Managers with Psychopathic Tendencies Make Worse Investors," Personality and Social Psychology Bulletin, October 19, 2017).

So perhaps being a jerk at the office is not the ticket to the corporate boardroom after all. An article in the Harvard Business Review concluded that "collectively, the research shows that creating a leadership model of trust and mutual cooperation may help create a culture that is happier, in which employees help each other, and consequently become more productive in the long run"

(Emma Seppala, "The Hard Data on Being a Nice Boss," Harvard Business Review, November 24, 2014).

Principle #12: Be Kind, Show Love

"Love is patient, love is kind. It does not envy, it does not boast, it is not proud. It does not dishonor others, it is not self-seeking, it is not easily angered, it keeps no record of wrongs. Love does not delight in evil but rejoices with the truth. It always protects, always trusts, always hopes, always perseveres." (1 Corinthians 13:4–7, New International Version).

"But love your enemies, do good to them, and lend to them without expecting to get anything back. Then your reward will be great, and you will be children of the Most High, because he is kind to the ungrateful and wicked" (Luke 6:35, New International Version).

I would be shocked if Harvard Business School is instructing its students to "love your enemies" or to "lend to them without expecting anything back." But they should. Here's why: When you square off against your enemies at work or in business, you expend incredible energy in resentment, jealousy, and anger toward them. You become paranoid that your coworker or business rival is trying to somehow subvert you or cause you harm. Instead, if you decide to be kind to them, they will be so surprised, they won't initially know how to react. In all probability, unless you're working with a sociopath, they will reciprocate with kindness toward you. In the future, this person may be in a position to help you get promoted or make a positive recommendation about you to a boss or customer. By contrast, showing unkindness and vilifying the person to your coworkers, boss, and spouse will only further alienate that person from you and create a reason for them in turn to oppose you on the job or in business.

Yet some corporate leaders don't understand this principle at all. Recently, a major credit card company revamped its policies for account payments by its customers. For its most reliable, best customers, the company shortened the amount of time the customer was allowed to make her monthly payment by a week. If the payment was not made within this new shortened period, the company assessed a late penalty on its best customers.

On the contrary, the company did not impose the shortened periods and penalties upon its deadbeat and worst customers. The reason for punishing the company's best customers was simply to extract more fees from those customers who paid the least interest and late fees. The worst customers were already paying higher interest and late fees.

Obviously, these reliable "best" customers will now be incentivized to move their accounts to more reasonable creditors with longer billing cycles.

One of the best examples of "loving your enemy" on a macro scale is the treatment of the "enemies" of the United States after World War II. In the aftermath of vanquishing both imperial Japan and Hitler's Germany, the economies and infrastructure of both nations were destroyed by the ravages of the fighting. However, the US did not punish these nations with sanctions, penalties, or mass incarcerations of their citizens. Instead, America allocated billions of dollars of American taxpayer dollars to rebuild and restore its economy into the powerhouse that they are today. In turn, the United States established them as trading partners with markets for US goods from the 1950s until today. America could have bitterly exacted revenge with justification against Japan for attacking the US at Pearl Harbor in 1941, killing three thousand Americans and starting a horrible war. Similarly, retribution against Nazi Germany would have been totally understood for the monstrous deeds of

Adolf Hitler and the murder of six million Jewish people in the Holocaust. Instead, America, in wisdom and with the ultimate act of forgiveness, restored these nations. As a result, neither Germany nor Japan has been an enemy of the US ever since.

Conversely, the Allies, including the US, England, France, and other nations, attempted to "punish" Germany after defeating that country in World War I. Germany was saddled with extreme financial debts to the Allied victors imposed under the Treaty of Versailles. As a result, Germany was bankrupted, and the German economy crashed under the weight of runaway inflation in the 1920s and early 1930s. This economic chaos led to the bitterness and resentment of the German people, giving rise to the empowerment of Adolf Hitler and World War II.

As it turns out, being kind only encourages reciprocity from your coworkers and rivals. If you are seriously networking with other businesspeople, it only makes sense that others will respond best to a warm welcome and a generous deed.

Be Kind, Show Love: Actions for Follow-Up, Week #12

#1: When have you acted kindly and shown love to someone who may have treated you unfairly? Did that person change their attitude toward you? When you identified someone as your rival, enemy, or someone you did not like, what acts of unkindness did you show them? How did they respond? If you have ever worked in a call center as a customer service rep, you have been instructed to respond in kindness and with respect to callers who are often mean, angry, and disrespectful to you. Perhaps the caller has been on hold for twenty-five minutes after getting a cell phone bill with unauthorized charges. That has happened to me. I must admit to not acting like a kind, patient Christian when I finally was able to speak to someone. Yet the customer rep treated me with kindness and respect, which I certainly didn't deserve. Consequently, I settled down and reciprocated with kindness and decency in response. (I had to repent of my bad attitude when I got off the phone!).

#2: Whom do you need to show kindness to today? Make a list. Don't just list the people who can potentially help you in your career and business. Perhaps you acted unkindly to the janitor or someone else whom you may think will never be in a position to assist you. Nevertheless, treat everyone with the same level of kindness. People around you will see the change in your attitude, and you will be blessed. Surprisingly, those whom you may think could never assist you in your job or business may indeed do just that. Quite a few years ago, I befriended a man at our church who was unemployed and needed to support his family. We needed some painting done at our home. Although he was inexperienced, I hired the man to help him financially to take care of his family. A few years later, he received a large sum of money in an insurance settlement. He was aware that I was a financial advisor. He called me and asked me to manage the funds for his family.

#3: What obstacles do you foresee that may prevent you from being kind and showing love at work and in your business? Toward your spouse and children? For example, do you fear that coworkers, business associates, or your spouse or kids will take advantage of you if you are kind to them?

#4: What sacrifices will you need to make to show kindness to coworkers, business associates, and family members? Do you fear losing business to a rival if you are kind to them? Are you concerned that being kind to your coworkers may result in them getting ahead of you? With your family, are you worried that you simply don't have the time to spend reaching out to them if they don't immediately respond to you as you wish?

#5: Looking back in one, five, and ten years from now, imagine that you don't show any more kindness toward coworkers, business associates, and family. What will your career, business, and family life look like? Could you be stuck in a lonely, dead-end job as a result of your own selfishness? Could you possibly be divorced? What will your relationship with your adult kids look like?

#6: Today, go out and be kind to at least one person at work and to a family member. How does it feel? Was it difficult for you? Get in the habit of doing this daily.

#7: If you are a believer, ask God to assist you in changing your attitude both at home and on the job. Focus on the principle of reciprocity. With the exception of sociopaths, most people will respond positively to your kind acts.

Chapter 17
Week #13
Principle: PATIENCE

Being Patient vs. Being Impulsive and Impatient

"Impulsive individuals make risky choices, motivated more by immediate reward than potential long-term negative consequences." (Impulsivity in Decision-Making: An Event-Related Potential Investigation, National Library of Medicine, National Center for Biotechnology Information, 2/2/2009).

For an entrepreneur, impatience may appear to be an asset. A hard-charger with a fast-paced modus operandi and the energy required to start a new business often comes bootstrapped with impatience and impulsivity.

Yet jumping to a conclusion and pushing a customer or a business partner to make a quick deal can also make you appear desperate. The result might be losing the deal or losing your partner. Obviously, impulsivity in business can cost you as well. Taking the first offer may result in paying too much or agreeing to contract terms that are onerous.

Principle #13: Be Patient

"But they that wait upon the Lord shall renew their strength; they shall mount up with wings as eagles; they shall run, and not be weary; and they shall walk, and not faint" (Isaiah 40:31, KJV).

"Rest in the Lord; wait patiently for him to act. Don't be envious of evil men who prosper. Stop your anger! Turn off your wrath. Don't fret and worry—it only leads to harm. For the wicked shall be destroyed." (Psalms 37:7–8, The Living Bible).

In the Bible, God told Abraham that he would "be the father of a multitude of nations" when he was already one hundred years old and his wife, Sarah, was ninety. However, later, Abraham and Sarah grew impatient, waiting for God to provide them a child. As a result, Abraham decided to produce a child through a sexual relationship with his slave Hagar. Thirteen years later, God fulfilled his promise to Abraham with the birth of Isaac to Sarah. Unfortunately, the child of Hagar, Ishmael, created chaos in Abraham's family. As a result, Hagar and Ishmael were banished to the desert. God was not pleased with Abraham's impatience.

Often, we see politicians, sports figures, and even church leaders who are dishonest. Many times, we have been appalled as we see them amassing incredible wealth. They may live in opulence, own a huge mansion, drive a Maserati, and travel around the world in a private jet. Here, the Lord is advising us not to become angry, resentful, and envious of their prosperity. Instead, we are called to be patient and "wait upon the Lord." God tells us to run and "not be weary." This simply means that our reward for persisting in doing the right thing is that we will not wear out, and "mounting up with wings," we will indeed succeed in our endeavors. Finally, those corrupt leaders in our culture will not ultimately succeed. They will be destroyed.

The need for patience is critical for success in business. Quite a few years ago, my wife, Cindy, and I owned a vacation home near Bend, Oregon. At least a couple weekends each month in the winter and for weeks at a time in the summer, we would take our kids and vacation there. The only drawback was the mortgage. We had figured that the appreciation in the value of the home would more than cover the dollars we spent paying the mortgage. We had planned to keep the home for our retirement. However, after almost six years, the home had not appreciated at all in value, and we were still paying a substantial mortgage. Consequently, we decided to sell the home and absorb the financial loss. However, within the next two years, the home was appreciating at a double-digit rate! If only we had been patient, we would have reaped a financial windfall in addition to vacationing at a place we loved.

A few years ago, a person I had known for several years owned a fireplace store and was building a very successful business. He was too eager to expand his business and open a chain of stores across the western states. Unfortunately, he was not patient. He borrowed several million dollars for his expansion. However, he had not checked into the market for his product, competition, and pricing in the other locations prior to opening the new stores. As a result, he was unable to repay his loans, and he was forced to declare bankruptcy.

Be Patient: Actions for Follow-Up, Week #13

#1: When have you exercised patience, and when has waiting on God paid off for you? If you're not a believer, when has patience led to a successful outcome for you? When have you acted impulsively with a bad or even disastrous outcome? For example, have you ever taken a lesser job because you lost patience waiting for the position you really wanted to be offered? Did you ever prematurely end a relationship with a boyfriend or girlfriend because you lost patience waiting for them to respond to you in the way you desired? Describe on paper.

#2: With whom can you show patience today? With your spouse? With your children? With your boss or a subordinate? Do you need to be patient about acquiring a certain house or car until you're able to budget for it?

#3: What obstacles in your life are preventing you from exercising patience? The Visa card in your wallet may be an obstacle to being patient with your finances and living within your income.

Perhaps one of your employees or a subordinate at work needs extra help in performing his or her job. What is preventing you from taking the time to help that person?

#4: What sacrifices must you make in order to be more patient? You may need to postpone a financial goal. If you wanted to buy that dream home in two years, perhaps you need to wait four years when you can better afford to make the payments. If you need to be more patient with your kids, you may just need to spend more time with them when you come home from work.

#5: If you continue to be impatient, looking back in one year, five years, and ten years, will you regret that you incurred a mountain of debt just to purchase something that you could have waited for? Will you regret your impatience with your husband or wife when they just needed you to listen to them? Your impatience may have cost you a job, a business, bankruptcy, or even a divorce.

#6: Today, be patient! Show your patience at the office, at home, and with your Visa card!

#7: Ask God to grant you patience in whatever you have determined is the Achilles heel of your impulsivity. Meditate upon the power of patience in your life and how you too will show patience and less impulsivity.

Chapter 18
Week #14
Principle: Compassion

Showing Compassion vs. Being Indifferent and Apathetic

Apathy will destroy the culture of your company, your business, and your family.

In my senior year of high school, my mother asked her friend to hire me to work part-time in the research department at the Baltimore Public Schools headquarters in downtown Baltimore. Mom had been working as an administrative assistant there for about ten years and had befriended the director of research. Initially, at age seventeen, I was excited about my new job. However, on the first day, I was led into a windowless room on an upper floor of an old building. The room not only was bereft of windows, but there were no pictures or decorations on the walls. Like soldiers in formation, gray secretary desks were lined up in rows of six apiece across the room. At each desk, a worker was seated with a box of old index cards in front of them. On the cards were old school records of students who had attended Baltimore schools many years prior in the 1940s and 1950s. Many of the cards were faded and difficult to read. My and my coworkers' job was to alphabetize the boxes of cards. When I completed alphabetizing one box of cards, I was simply to refile it and get another box of cards.

Fortunately, I worked only a four-hour part-time shift, Monday to Friday. My coworkers were mostly older women who sat at their desks alphabetizing cards from 8:00 a.m. to 5:00 p.m., Monday through Friday. There were no other tasks to be performed. Our supervisor, a man in his mid-thirties, would occasionally come into our room, talk to one or two employees, and go away. After working there only one day, I sensed the apathy and futility of my fellow workers. It was contagious. By the end of my first week there, I absolutely hated the job, and I looked at my watch every ten minutes. Our manager made zero effort to commiserate with the plight of his employees, many of whom had worked there for several years at low pay with prison-like working conditions. There was no attempt to acknowledge or reward employees for exceptional performance. In fact, there was no way to measure performance. No one counted how many boxes of cards I alphabetized, or even if I had alphabetized them correctly. For all they knew, I could have filed names starting with Z ahead of the A's! Apathy and indifference by management had spread to the workforce. Employees were falling asleep at their desks and spending an inordinate amount of time in the bathroom.

Earlier, we cited a Gallup poll which tried to determine if US employees feel engaged in their work (Jim Harter, "Employee Engagement on the Rise in U.S.," Gallup, August 26, 2018, www.gallup.com). The results of this Poll are truly shocking. "Engagement at work" for the purpose of this poll included whether the employees were at all encouraged by a supervisor or manager in their work. Also, the poll asked workers whether they thought their opinion mattered in the workplace. Finally, Gallup included whether the employees felt they could do what they do best every day. Conversely, engaged employees were described as those who were involved in, enthusiastic about, and committed to their jobs. The vast majority of employees did not feel encouraged by their managers and did not feel that their opinions mattered to their employers. Finally, most employees did not feel that their bosses enabled them to perform at their best each day.

This lack of engagement at work can be easily extrapolated to your family. If Dad and Mom are too busy with long hours at work and watching TV in the evening, they can expect their children to be "disengaged" from the family. If your children don't receive encouragement at home and don't believe their opinions matter in the family, they are going to be apathetic and indifferent the next time you take them to the beach.

Principle #14: Be Compassionate to Others

"Be kind and compassionate to one another, forgiving each other, just as in Christ, God forgave you." (Ephesians 4:32, NIV).

"If anyone has material possessions and sees a brother or sister in need but has no pity on them, how can the love of God be in that person?" (1 John 3:17, NIV).

"Science also supports the upside of compassion. In their review of research on compassion at work, Dutton and colleagues highlight that being treated with compassion at work produces positive emotions, reduces anxiety, and strengthens an employee's commitment to and gratitude towards the organization. In compassionate climates, people also feel valued, to the point that managers who act compassionately are perceived as more convincing and effective leaders" ("How Compassion Can Benefit Your Business, Forbes, October 13, 2020).

It only stands to reason that where companies focus on very short-term revenue goals in a high-pressure environment, the employer will experience more absenteeism, greater health care costs, and higher employee turnover as a result of a less loyal workforce. Consequently, as a manager, a business owner, or an employee, showing and receiving compassion is simply good for you and your company.

When I was starting out in sales, a salesman in the next office was a conscientious worker but a poor salesman. As a result, every Friday, the branch manager would march into his cubicle within earshot of the entire office staff. The manager would verbally harangue the man, shouting at him in a profanity-laced tirade for his failure to achieve an assigned quota of sales. The manager exhibited absolutely no compassion or kindness. After several months of the manager's ruthless behavior, he fired the employee, again within earshot of the rest of us. As you would expect, the manager lost the respect and loyalty of the staff, and he himself was eventually let go.

In the business world, a positive sign in our culture today is the visibility of companies displaying their compassion by means of donations to charity and efforts to assist their employees. Starbucks publicized efforts to assist its baristas with college tuition. This type of employee scholarship is bound to boost worker morale, loyalty, and productivity. Of course, the display of "compassion" may often in part reflect a corporation's intention to avoid the added costs of their employees forming a union.

Show Compassion to Others: Actions for Follow-Up, Week #14

#1: When have you shown compassion to someone in the past and later reaped an unexpected benefit from doing so? In your family, do you see compassion reciprocated on a daily basis with your spouse and children? When have you been rude to someone at work, and what was the result?

#2: Whom can you show compassion to at work? At home? Think of someone you can show compassion to who cannot possibly ever repay you. Compassion may simply be a word of encouragement to your boss or coworker. It may include bringing home a dozen roses or playing basketball with your son when you really feel like taking a nap.

#3: What obstacles prevent you from being compassionate at work? Do you feel that your time is too valuable during the workday to assist someone who may be going through a divorce or who is stressed out? When you come home, are you too tired to listen to your spouse tell you about his or her day?

#4: What sacrifices will you need to make in order to become a more compassionate coworker, spouse, boss, or business owner? For example, to show compassion as a lifestyle, you may help out at a food bank or church or make a regular financial contribution to a charity. In your job, perhaps you can start a weekly Bible study. At home, you can schedule an evening devotion time with your spouse and kids. If you are not a believer, you can volunteer at a secular charity and conduct a family movie or game night. All these efforts require a sacrifice of your time.

#5: If you decide not to adopt a lifestyle of compassion for others, consider how you will feel in ten years. Will you regret your lack of kindness? Will your relationships at work or home suffer?

#6: Today, show compassion to one person at work and to a family member at home. Make this a daily habit and commitment. Write it down. Also, track the short- and, later, the longer-term results of showing compassion daily.

#7: Ask God to help you develop a daily calendar for showing compassion, including for the person to whom you will direct your kindness each day. Also, ask the Lord which charity you should be donating to. Also, review your values and determine which charities best represent those values. Make your donation accordingly.

Chapter 19
Week #15
Principle: Be RELIABLE

Being Reliable vs. Being Undependable and Risky

When I was a teenager, my mom would occasionally shop at a large retail store called Montgomery Ward. Montgomery Ward sold just about everything. You could buy a new watch, a new suit, or a lawn mower and TV there. Their prices were usually very competitive, and I would describe them as being similar to Walmart in many respects. However, unlike Walmart, Costco, and many online retailers today, Montgomery Ward suffered from a reputation with customers for being unreliable. Mom told me about her frustrations with late deliveries, sending the wrong items, and incorrectly charging her account. Other times, Wards delivered the package, and it was broken. Montgomery Ward went out of business in December 2000, in large part because it could not be counted on.

Many years later, I was serving as Executive Assistant Superintendent of the Oregon State Police. One of our state troopers was only a year or two away from retirement. This trooper had been an extremely reliable and effective employee for many years. However, while working the graveyard shift from one of our small offices, he unfortunately became embroiled in a sexual affair with a female dispatcher in the office when he should have been out patrolling and protecting the citizens. As a result, we were compelled to discharge him after more than twenty years with our department. Lack of reliability in the end cost this gentleman his full retirement.

Many of us have worked for an unreliable boss. This could be a boss who lied to you, demeaned you behind your back, couldn't articulate his expectations for you, or simply created a hostile or indifferent workplace. Hiring an unreliable manager will undoubtedly result in high rates of employee attrition, a recent study found. Fifty-seven percent of workers in a recent survey stated that they had quit a job because of a bad boss ("Employees, Really Do Leave Bad Bosses, Research Shows," Dive Brief, HR Dive, December 11, 2019, https://www.hrdive.com/news/employees-really-do-leave-bad-bosses-research-shows/56877)).

For a number of years, I battled with a problem of being chronically late for appointments with my clients and office meetings, and even meeting my wife for dinner. Only by consistently applying myself to develop the habit of being on time have I mostly overcome this bad habit. I learned that the root of the problem was my repeated underestimation of how long it would take to get to my meetings. To solve the problem, I started doubling the time I would allow for travel to each meeting. I have since also discovered that many other people who struggle with lateness also chronically underestimate their travel time. I recommend this remedy of doubling your travel time if you suffer from the same chronic delusion I did! That way, you will arrive early even if you need to stop for gas, run into heavy traffic, or have trouble finding a parking space when you arrive.

Being late is an insult to the person you are meeting with. You're saying that your time is valuable, but their time is not. I am also grateful for my cell phone. Now, at least, when I am running late, I make certain to call ahead and let the person know I will not be there on time and give them the option of rescheduling the appointment.

Of course, this principle also extends to your family. Your spouse and your kids need to know they can rely upon you as a mother, father, husband, or wife for consistency, honesty, commitment, and compassion.

Principle #15 - Be Reliable

"But whoever keeps his word, in him truly the love of God is perfected" (1 John 2:5, ESV).

What does "keeping your word" entail? First, if your employer requires you to show up at 8:00 a.m. for work, you agree to that condition of employment when you accept your job. Arriving at 8:05 a.m. is not keeping your word.

Certainly, in business, keeping your word means meeting a deadline your boss sets for completion of a project. It may also mean not lying to your boss when he or she asks you how much progress you have made to date.

Following company policy, paying attention to the little details, and being a team player all fall under the rubric of dependability for any business.

If you own the business and you are obligated to perform a contract for your client, it means not making the excuse that you are too busy to get it done on time, your key employee quit, or you need the client to pay more money to complete the job.

In a marriage and family, being dependable means you abide by your marital vows. You don't engage in extramarital affairs. You don't make excuses for not being available when your children need you. If they have a baseball game, you show up regardless of an argument you had with your boss or your spouse that morning.

Finally, your company and your family should be able to rely upon you to take the initiative. For example, if your employer is requesting new ideas in your sphere of influence in the workplace, you should be thinking, developing, and generating those ideas. If someone needs to plan the family vacation, your spouse should be able to count on you,

"His lord said to him, 'Well done, good and faithful servant; you were faithful over a few things, I will make you ruler over many things." (Matthew 25:21, NKJV).

In my financial planning practice, many retired clients rely upon the monthly check we send them from their investment portfolio to pay their bills. On one occasion, an elderly lady called me on a Monday morning to chastise me for not having received her monthly check on the prior Friday. I checked, and we had mailed the check to her on the prior Wednesday. I naively and smugly informed her that the "check was in the mail and," and the reason she hadn't received her money on time was obviously due to the incompetence of the US Postal Service, not me. She promptly uttered a few four-letter words, hung up, and transferred her account to another investment firm. That day, I learned a hard lesson in both being reliable and not passing the buck. Starting the following month, my assistant and I started sending out our client's checks an additional week in advance each month to account for the possibility (or probability!) of slow mail delivery.

Here, the Bible is telling us that if we are dependable in our job or business, we will be promoted and experience greater responsibility and success in the future. This is a true prosperity gospel based upon the Puritan work ethic. There is no magic to this. It does not matter if you are a believer or nonbeliever, for you to reap the benefit of being reliable in your job or business.

Be Reliable: Actions for Follow-Up, Week #15

#1: How have you displayed reliability in your job, in your business, and with your family in the past? What benefits have you received from your diligence? When have you failed to be dependable, and what negative consequences were a result? Make a list of both.

#2: In what specific behavior at work or home can you display dependability where you currently are not totally reliable? For example, if you're chronically late for work, list this behavior. If you tend to neglect important details in completing projects or you fail to take the initiative, add these behaviors to your list.

#3: What obstacles stand in the way of your being more dependable now? One roadblock to dependability is that it's inconvenient for you. Dependability requires that you place the needs of others ahead of yours. Whether it be for your boss, your spouse, your company, or your kids, you won't become more dependable until you prioritize their needs ahead of your own.

#4: What sacrifices will you need to make to start being more dependable? If you tend to be a loner at work, you may need to surrender that behavior and become more of a team player. If you habitually circumvent company policy because doing things your way is faster, you may need to give that behavior up in favor of following the rules.

#5: If you don't become a more reliable employee, business owner, or spouse, will you be trapped in a dead-end job, a stagnant business, or a poor relationship with your husband or wife in ten years?

#6: Use the list of behaviors you vowed to improve upon in day #2 to start changing today! You may need to spend several weeks focusing on your unreliable behaviors and developing new habits.

#7: Ask the Lord to assist you in becoming more dependable in each behavior you listed. Meditate upon your list, start making the changes, and know that increasing your dependability can bring you the promotions, business opportunities, and family cohesiveness you desire.

Chapter 20
Week #16
SELF-DISCIPLINE

Exercising Self-Discipline vs. Being Disorganized and Slothful

Disorganization and sloth destroy productivity, erode employee morale, and cripple time management. Customers and clients can readily detect when your business is disorganized and lackadaisical. Obviously, a reputation for disorganization and sloth in customer service may fatally damage your brand, whether you're a sole proprietor or a large corporation.

"An Express Employment Professionals survey of more than 18,000 business leaders showed that 57% of Respondents said they lose six work hours per week due to disorganization. The survey also found that disorganized employees who make $50,000 annually cost their companies about $11,000 per year in lost time due to their disorganization." (Julie Perrine, "The Struggle is Real: Disorganization Can Cost You," Executive Support Magazine, November 25, 2015). The National Association of Professional Organizers says we spend one year of our lives looking for lost items. Office workers waste an average of 40 percent of their workday due to disorganization (Sherry Borsheim, "Organization and Time Management Statistics," Simply Productive, March 12, 2012).

Unfortunately, we are paying a steep price for our utter lack of self-discipline in business. However, this also carries over to our families on the home front. Eighty percent of the clutter in your home is a result of disorganization, not lack of space (Sherry

Borsheim, "Organization and Time Management Statistics," Simply Productive, March 12, 2012). Surprisingly, 23 percent of adults pay bills late and incur fees because they can't find their bills. ("Household Clutter is Costing You a Bundle," Forbes.com, March 28, 2017).

I find this statistic on bill-paying amusing in that today, most of us pay our bills online. However, I plead guilty to sometimes having lost passwords and websites for my bills. Occasionally, as a result, I paid a few bills late. Consequently, once I was determined to become totally organized, I made a list of all my bill websites and passwords, so I no longer need to click the "forgot password" button on my laptop.

Principle #16: Establish Your Self-Discipline

"For God hath not given us the spirit of fear; but of power, and of love, and of a sound mind." (2 Timothy, 1:17 KJV).

Fear is indeed the greatest obstacle to self-discipline in most people's lives.

Self-discipline simply means your willingness to do the things you don't like to do in order to achieve the results you desire. Most people are unwilling to engage in behaviors they don't like in order to achieve their longer-term goals. When I started out as a stockbroker, I was told that I had to make a minimum of fifty cold calls on the telephone each day to be successful. This required me to phone and talk with at least fifty different people each day to solicit them to open an account and purchase a stock or bond. At that time in the nineties, cold calling was virtually the only way to build a successful financial advisory business. Once built, the business would net a stockbroker a substantial six-figure income, and cold-calling would no longer be required. However, on average, only about 5 percent of new stockbrokers were still in the business after five years! This means that 95 percent of them were unwilling to put up with people who hung up the phone, cursed them out, or just said, "I'm not interested." However, the 5 percent who were self-disciplined established an amazing business and income for life!

Self-discipline is impossible without long-term goals and planning. Most people lack self-discipline because they fail to establish goals. You might dream of piloting a Boeing 747 for United Airlines. However, unless you set that as your long-term goal, establish short-term bridge goals, and set up a plan to reach each short-term goal, you will never develop the self-discipline to become that 747 pilot. For example, you would need to get a bachelor's degree for most airlines to hire you. That would be your first short-term goal. When you're saving to pay your tuition, studying for final exams, and spending long hours in the library, you need to see yourself reaching the goal of flying that jet. Otherwise, you won't be sufficiently motivated to reach that prerequisite to becoming a pilot.

Despite our nation's debt, relative to the world, America is still awash in wealth. I reviewed a study recently revealing that there are only three goals Americans need to achieve to avoid poverty. These are:

1) Graduate from High School

2) Obtain a full-time job

3) Get married (and don't have kids before you do!)

According to this study, 97% of millennials who can accomplish this will not suffer poverty. ("What does the success sequence mean?" Bryan Caplan, Institute for Family Studies, ifstudies.org/blog (2/25/21)). Of course, our goal is not to just avoid poverty. However, for many people who are not pursuing true prosperity, this will suffice for them.

Reaching our Goals

"For God has not given us a spirit of fear and timidity, but of power, love, and self-discipline." (2 Timothy 1:7, NLT). This verse in Timothy is telling us that God has given us "a spirit of power" to reach our goals. However, it doesn't say that God has made it easy for us. On the contrary, 2 Timothy is anticipating our "fear" and advising us that "fear" is not from God. We are afraid for two reasons: (1) We fear that we won't be strong enough to endure the undesirable hard work it will take to reach our goal. (2) We fear that even after laboring to reach our objective, we will fail anyway. Consequently, only confidence in God and our eventual success will enable us to discipline ourselves to accomplish the difficult tasks that lead to accomplishing our goals.

Perhaps the most important key to developing your self-discipline is the establishment of both short-term and long-term goals. First, the goal must be important enough that you are willing to prioritize it. Second, the goal must not be too easy to achieve. If your goal is to simply get a job and you have a high school diploma, you should be able to achieve that goal with a minimum-wage job at a fast-food restaurant within a week or two. If you're a high school student, that might be a legitimate goal. If you've already graduated, then it might be a very short-term goal until you can get a better-paying job. If your goal is to become a physician, your short-term goal might be to get your bachelor's degree. You might also set a goal of achieving a certain grade point average, i.e., 3.8, to be accepted to medical school. The next goal would be to actually get accepted into medical school, and finally, a goal to graduate from medical school.

However, the goal also must eventually be achievable. If your goal is to be a billionaire in five years and you have only $10,000 now, you might want to modify that goal. Perhaps you could focus on starting a business and building a net worth of $1 million in ten years. Again, you will need to break the long-term goal of $1 million down to maybe a short-term goal of $500,000 in five years and to have your new business running in two years.

You should review your goals at least monthly. Be flexible. Revise and modify your goals when necessary. In the example above, you may find it takes six years to achieve $500,000. Revise your short- and long-term goals accordingly. However, never give up on your long-term goals. These goals should reflect your ultimate dreams. If your goal is indeed financial, what will you accomplish for the Kingdom of God when you achieve it? Building yourself a vacation home in the Bahamas and a ski hut in Aspen should not be the main purpose for your labor in life.

Finally, it is virtually impossible to develop your self-discipline unless your self-discipline is pointed toward the attainment of a long-term goal. For example, if I tell my son he needs to run two miles every morning, he will immediately ask me why. If I say, "Well, it's simply a good habit to develop self-discipline," he will think I'm just trying to torture him. Yet if he needs to lose weight, I can tell him to set a goal for his weight, and running will enable him to achieve it. If he wants to be successful in basketball, his running will help to set the goal of competitive endurance, so when it's the fourth quarter of the basketball game and other players are beginning to tire, he will outperform.

In summary, goal achievement requires self-discipline as much as self-discipline requires goals. Your self-discipline will set you apart from the masses of people who lack motivation, direction, and discipline.

Self-Discipline: Actions for Follow-Up, Week #16

#1: When have you exercised self-discipline in the past to reach a financial, educational, or business-related goal? For example, you might have set a goal to be accepted at a certain college or university. What steps did you need to take to attain that goal? When did your failure to exercise self-discipline result in your personal failure?

#2: What goals do you need to establish, and what self-discipline will that require of you? Where in your life today are you failing to exercise self-discipline? For example, this may include your attempts to lose weight, find a better job, or save money.

#3: What obstacles are preventing you from exercising self-discipline in your life today? Perhaps you have envisioned yourself owning a new home with a swimming pool. However, you have initiated no action to fulfill that dream. Turn that dream into a real goal. Now you must go on Zillow and find homes with pools that you would desire to own. Find out the price, the approximate down payment needed, and what the total monthly outlay, including taxes, for the home would be. Now you are prepared to set the purchase of the home with a pool as a goal. Depending on your finances, this might be a two-year, five-year, or seven-year goal. Calculate how much you will need to save monthly and how much employment income you need annually. Then you will be prepared to exercise self-discipline. This will entail setting aside so much per month in savings and finding a higher-paying job to pay the mortgage. Again, these are the short-term bridge goals toward achieving your long-term goal. In any event, whatever steps you need to take in order to accomplish the long-term goal will represent your self-discipline.

#4: What sacrifices will you need to make to achieve the self-discipline that will carry you to your long-term goal? If your goal is to lose forty pounds, list all the foods you will need to give up to achieve this objective. Then list the exercise routine and its frequency and duration needed to burn the calories to lose weight. Next, the most difficult part will be the self-discipline required to retain the regimen for the rest of your life.

#5: If you fail to develop self-discipline in the next five years, how will you feel when you have not reached the dreams and goals you wanted to achieve? Will you regret having not sacrificed now to enjoy the fruits of your labor later?

#6: Today is the first day of your new regimen of self-discipline to achieve your goal. What goal are you establishing for yourself? What will you start doing today to achieve it? What time period are you permitting yourself to accomplish your goal? What short-term bridge goals will be required, and what period are you establishing for those short-term bridge goals? Write down each long-term goal and its deadline. Write down each short-term goal and its deadline. Enumerate the steps of self-discipline you are taking to reach your goals on a daily basis.

#7: Pray for self-discipline and vision to make the sacrifices now for the vision of achieving your long-term goals. Meditate upon your own reservoir of self-confidence, your vision for the future, and your willingness to make the sacrifice to accomplish your objectives.

Chapter 21
Week #17
Principle: SERVANT LEADERSHIP

Being a Servant Leader vs. Being an Autocratic Leader

Autocratic leaders look out for themselves and may be indifferent to the welfare of their subordinates. Autocrats make decisions without consulting their subordinates or other group members. The result is often a lack of support from within the group, low morale, and the inability to find creative solutions to problems without group advice and consensus. Russian President Vladimir Putin exemplifies this leadership style. The invasion of Ukraine, a sovereign nation, without support from its advisors, its military, or the majority of the Russian people, typifies this approach. As his military offensive bogged down in Ukraine, protests from Russian citizens, military desertions, and the resignation of key officials revealed the failure of this leadership style.

In today's workplace, this authoritarian management style will not work, especially with the millennial generation. "Research shows that the work environment, how one is treated, and if one is allowed to speak up and be heard are most important. Unless someone is in pure survival mode, you can't hold on to them (employees) by throwing more money at them" (Mark Robertson, " Why Authoritarian Leadership Doesn't Work Anymore," Forbes, February 14, 2019).

When your workers are dispirited by your top-down bossiness, they will spend their shifts complaining to coworkers and looking for a new job. Your company's productivity will tank, and you will waste your otherwise productive time reviewing employment applications, interviewing new hires, and training new employees.

Principle #17: Being a Servant Leader

"Jesus called them together and said, 'You know that those who are regarded as rulers of the Gentiles lord it over them, and their high officials exercise authority over them. Not so with you. Instead, whoever wants to become great among you must be your servant" (Mark 10:42–43, NIV).

"Sitting down, Jesus called the Twelve and said, 'Anyone who wants to be first must be the very last, and the servant of all.'" (Mark 9:35, NIV).

The Lord turns the business school's model upside down. If you want to be the CEO, be the servant. This means you always place the needs of your employees ahead of your own. We see the opposite behavior in many of our corporate CEOs today. In 2020, the average CEO of an S&P 500 publicly traded company received a total compensation of $15.5 million per year. The ratio of the average CEO to worker pay was 299 to 1. (www.aflcio.org/executive-paywatch/company-pay-ratios) 2020.

Can you imagine Jesus earning 299 times what his disciples earned? He is telling us to set an example of frugality and humility as a leader. Jesus washed the feet of his disciples. How many corporate CEO's do you see washing their employees' feet?

John 13:12–17 (NIV) describes Jesus washing the disciples' feet:

When he had finished washing their feet, he put on his clothes and returned to his place. "Do you understand what I have done for you?" he asked them. "You call me 'Teacher' and 'Lord,' and rightly so, for that is what I am. Now that I, your Lord, and Teacher, have washed your feet, you also should wash one another's feet. I have set you an example that you should do as I have done for you. Very truly I tell you, no servant is greater than his master, nor is a messenger greater than the one who sent him. Now that you know these things, you will be blessed if you do them."

Jesus's washing of the disciples' feet represents the mindset you should have as a CEO, a middle manager, or a line supervisor. If overtime work is required, you should be there with your subordinates. If the company loses money, you should be the first to take the pay cut. If your employee is sick and runs out of sick leave, you should donate your own sick leave. If you are the CEO, you should be constantly looking out for opportunities to sacrifice part of your own compensation to assist the family of an employee who may be injured or sick. The servant leader leads by example.

"Recent research in the area suggests that servant leadership behaviors are associated with positive outcomes such as enhanced employee organizational commitment, creativity, organizational citizenship behaviors (OCBs), and job performance (e.g., Ehrhart, 2004). According to new research from Emlyon Business School in France, not only does servant leadership improve employee morale, but it also increases company profit" ("How Servant Leaders Boost Profits and Employee Morale," Forbes, July 15, 2020).

Examples of servant leadership include Martin Luther King Jr., Abraham Lincoln, and Mother Teresa. On the corporate level, Starbucks and Chick-fil-A have been described as corporate examples of servant leadership. Servant leaders are great listeners, show empathy for their employees' needs, and use the power of persuasion rather than using their authority to dominate and intimidate their subordinates.

Mother Teresa set up soup kitchens, a leper colony, orphanages, and a home for the dying and destitute. She treated the lepers, educated the poorest of the poor, and fed the homeless. She treated them like her family. While she set up 623 missions in 123 countries, she herself helped people individually who were suffering from leprosy, HIV, and tuberculosis (https://sites.psu.edu/leadership/2013/11/09/a-true-servant-leader-mother-teresa).

This is true servant leadership.

Servant Leadership: Actions for Follow-Up, Week #17

#1: When have you been a servant leader in the past, and how has it worked out for you? If you're not a boss or supervisor, have you exercised servant leadership with your kids and spouse? What was the result? When have you failed to show servant leadership at work, and how could you have achieved a better result as a servant leader?

#2: What areas of your work and family life can be improved now by exercising servant leadership? Could you be more productive by using the principles of servant leadership in your job? Your business? Your family life? Make a list.

#3: What obstacles do you foresee that would prevent you from exercising servant leadership at work? At home? As a middle manager or supervisor, you may need to petition your boss to allow you to adopt a servant leadership approach. The incentive for the business owner, of course, is improved productivity and employee loyalty. As a business owner, you may fear short-term productivity losses if you're not confident that servant leadership actually works. As a parent, you may incorrectly fear the loss of control over your children if you display servant leadership with them. For example, if your teenager's job is to take out the trash, why not help him or her? The obstacle may be your own pridefulness.

#4: What sacrifices will you need to make in order to exercise servant leadership? If you're a business owner, there may be a change in your regimen for your company that could result in a short-term loss of productivity in exchange for longer-term growth and increased productivity. If you become a servant leader at home, the extra time helping your children or doing chores your spouse normally does will require a sacrifice of some of your free time in exchange for better relationships.

#5: When you look back on today in ten years, will you regret not having improved your relationships at work and at home by not being a servant leader? As a business leader, did you lose good employees you might have retained as a servant leader? As a parent, would your relationships with your children and your husband or wife be much better today if you had exercised servant leadership?

#6: Begin taking the initiative today to be a servant leader with your subordinates at work and your spouse and kids at home. How does it feel to make a major positive change in your relationships? Outline in writing what steps you are taking to exercise servant leadership both at home and at work.

#7: Pray that your servant leadership will set an example for your coworkers and your spouse and kids. Have confidence that you're embarking on a new, positive chapter in your life that will promote your career and enhance your family relationships.

Chapter 22
Week #18
Principle: GRATITUDE

Being Grateful vs. Being Unthankful and Greedy

When we are unthankful for our blessings, it is generally because we are discontented and greedy for more. Often ungrateful people are also angry and resentful over their lack of what they feel they are entitled to and what they see others having acquired. Research conducted by the Harvard Business Review analyzed the effects of anger on decision-making, concluding that holding onto resentment and anger throughout the day will poison choices made and actions taken (Jennifer S. Lerner, "How Anger Poisons Decision Making," Harvard Business Review, September 2010).

It makes sense that when we covet what someone else has accomplished or his or her possessions, we are often stressed and unhappy. In a frame of mind of negativity and anger, our vision is clouded, and we are inclined to make poor decisions.

Does child abuse come from that same attitude of ingratitude? Parents who abuse their kids are generally angry and resentful toward them. If they were thankful for the son or daughter God has blessed them with, would they be inclined to abuse that child?

Don't we see wars started over an unthankful attitude? Germany started World War II over Hitler's greed for land, power, and resources. He and Germany's leaders were not content with the wealth of their nation. Saddam Hussein invaded Kuwait because he was greedy and coveted their oil.

Principle #18: Be Grateful

"I will give thanks to you, Lord, with all my heart. I will tell of all your wonderful deeds" (Proverbs 9:1).

"Enter his gates with thanksgiving and his courts with praise; give thanks to him and praise his name, for the Lord is good and his love endures forever." (Proverbs 100:4–5, NIV).

"In its in-depth 2019 Global Happiness and Well-Being Policy Report, the Global Happiness Council estimated that 'a meaningful increase in well-being' yields, on average, about a 10% increase in productivity" (Eric Mosley, "The Business Impact of Gratitude," Forbes, November 27, 2019).

So being thankful to God makes you more productive and successful in your work, business, and family!

Gratitude is also important for your mental health. "Studies show practicing gratitude can lead to more intimate and connected relationships, less depression, more motivation and engagement, and better overall mental well-being" (New York-Presbyterian, "Is Gratitude Good for Your Health?" Health Matters, 2022).

People like to associate with, talk to, and be friends with you when you're positive and thankful. It's truly not possible to be thankful and to constantly complain, criticize, and be negative. Thanking God for your good fortune is an acknowledgement that it's not all about you.

Gratitude is also a key to better physical health.

"One recent study found that people who were more grateful actually had better heart health, specifically less inflammation and healthier heart rhythms." (Lauren Dunn, "Be Thankful, Science Says Gratitude is good for your Health," University of California,

San Diego School of Medicine, The Today Show, November 26, 2015).

Thankfulness is difficult in our consumer culture today. Television commercials, internet ads, family, and friends all push us to be dissatisfied with our cars, clothing, houses, and restaurants. We need newer cars, bigger homes, fancier restaurants, and higher-end clothes. We are urged to use credit card debt, consumer loans, and maxed-out debt on our mortgages to temper our dissatisfaction with what we have.

Whether you're a Christian or a nonbeliever, the enticements are the same. You must exercise the self-discipline we discussed in week #15 to avoid the trap of unhappiness caused by consumerism in our culture.

In the midst of benefiting from the greatest personal freedom, material wealth, and educational opportunities of any nation in history, we as Americans often behave as spoiled children of rich parents. Instead of displaying gratitude for our magnificent wealth and liberty, we are witnessing riots, violence, sexual promiscuity, and rebellion against both our nation and the biblical principles of Christianity. Certainly, America is still grappling with problems of race, poverty, and corruption. However, when viewed against the panorama of world history and the wickedness of Russian, Chinese, German, and Japanese totalitarianism since the mid-twentieth century, America remains the shining city upon the hill.

Be Grateful: Actions for Follow-Up, Week #18

#1: When were you grateful in the past? Were you thankful for your freedom? Your health? Your job and your income? Were you grateful for your husband or wife? Your children? Your friends? Make a list of who and what you have been thankful for in the past and how they made you feel. Recall specifically when you have been ungrateful for many of these blessings in your life. Were you anxious about, angry at, or resentful of others you perceived as more successful, healthier, or having a better marriage or relationship with their kids?

#2: Whom should you be thankful for in your life now? God? Your spouse? Your children? Friends? What can you be thankful for now? Your business? Your 401k plan? Your job? Your health? Your freedom? Make a list.

#3: What obstacles do you see in becoming more thankful? Typical excuses include "I don't have time for that," "If I'm thankful, then I may not have the drive and ambition to push myself forward; I may become complacent," and "I'm a self-made man/woman; I don't owe a debt of gratitude to anybody."

#4: What sacrifices do you need to make in order to be more thankful? You may need to give up a bitter, critical, and/or negative attitude that has developed into a lifelong habit. You also may need to sacrifice making excuses when events do not turn out the way you want them to.

#5: If you remain unthankful for all the blessings in your life, when you look back in ten years, will you regret all the frustration, depression, and poor health you caused yourself by not showing gratitude for all the wonderful things in your life?

#6: Take your list from day #2 and start showing gratitude today! Find a quiet place in your home where you can take fifteen minutes and thank God for those items on your list. Next, start thanking your spouse, kids, and friends for your relationship by doing acts of kindness for each of them. This is not a one-time exercise. Each day, you should find at least one of these people to show gratitude toward. If you're a nonbeliever, you can be thankful to each person since you don't have God to thank. You can still be thankful for your income and job. At least thank the person who hired you or promoted you. Be grateful for the soldiers who died in battle for your personal freedom today. Of course, be always thankful for the mother and father who raised you. Remember, there is a special blessing in the Bible for honoring your parents: "Honor your father and mother." This is the first commandment, with a promise: if you honor your father and mother, "things will go well for you, and you will have a long life on the earth" (Ephesians 6:2–3, NLT).

#7: Ask the Lord to help you become a more thankful human being. Anytime you have asked God for wisdom, you have asked him for gratitude without knowing it. This is because thankfulness is wisdom. You should meditate upon all the wonderful people in your life and how they have helped you.

Chapter 23
Week #19
Principle: Mentoring

Mentoring Your Coworkers and Family vs. Being the Lone Ranger at the Office and at Home

Even the Lone Ranger had a mentee: Tonto!

Having allies in business is crucial to your success. Being a friend to a younger colleague is not only the morally right thing to do; it will provide your business with success as well. Mentoring a younger coworker or subordinate will increase your own learning. In order to teach, you must brush up on your own knowledge and skills. As far as being an entrepreneur mentee, being the recipient of advice from a mentor can increase your business revenue by as much as 83 percent (Brian Scudamore, "For Entrepreneurs: How to Avoid Lone-Wolf Syndrome," Forbes, September 26, 2016).

Research indicates that "lone wolves" lack organizational commitment. The lone wolf is the businessperson, entrepreneur, or employee who does not seek allies or their advice. They manage their business or their boss's business with little or no input from others. Also, they offer little or no assistance to junior coworkers, subordinates, or their boss. Their lack of commitment to the company should be a red flag about their inability to create added strength in the group through collaboration with other people. In sports, the opposite of the lone wolf is the player who, by virtue of his leadership, makes the other players on the team better. Tom Brady, NFL quarterback, exemplifies that team player. He has seven Super Bowl rings to prove the point. When he could have taken millions of dollars more in annual salary, he took less money so that other players on his team could be paid more. This enabled his team to acquire better players and allowed him to earn the respect and admiration of his teammates.

When your organization lacks mentors, the loss of continuity means that younger workers fail to learn the methodology, history, traditions, and culture necessary to support the branding you are known for. For example, if your company is known for superior personal customer service, a failure to mentor new employees results in a lack of appreciation for that behavior. Consequently, customers familiar with the connection between your company and superior service will start disassociating your brand with that level of customer service.

In your family, the loss of a mentor in America today is called a crisis of fatherlessness. "States with a lower percentage of single-parent families, on average, will have lower rates of juvenile crime. State-by-state analysis indicates that, in general, a 10 percent increase in the number of children living in single-parent homes (including divorces) accompanies a 17 percent increase in juvenile crime" ("Effects of Fatherless Families on Crime Rates," www. Marripedia.org). "Children from fatherless homes are more likely to be poor, become involved in drug and alcohol abuse, drop out of school, and suffer from health and emotional problems. Boys are more likely to become involved in crime, and girls are more likely to become pregnant as teens" ("The Consequences of Fatherlessness," www.Fathers.com).

Mentorship is just as imperative in the family as it is in your office.

Principle #19: Mentor Another Person

A mentor is a person who cares for you and who wants only the best for you. In the Bible, there are multiple examples of mentorship.

Abraham was a mentor to Isaac, Jacob was a mentor to Joseph, Moses mentored Joshua, and Elijah was a teacher and mentor to Elisha. Also, David, the father of King Solomon, advised and mentored his son.

"Teaching them to observe all things that I have commanded you." (Matthew 28:20, NKJV). In Matthew, Jesus tells his disciples to instruct the new believers in his teachings. Jesus mentored his disciples, whom he in turn expected to teach the new believers they brought to him. This mandate is reinforced in the Old Testament: "Give instruction to a wise man and he will be still wiser, teach a righteous man and he will increase his learning." (Proverbs 9:9, NKJV).

From a business standpoint, mentoring your assistant and junior managers develops your minor league farm team for future Senior Vice Presidents and CEOs for your company. Finally, altruistically, as a businessperson, senior executive, or technician, mentoring is a way for you to give back to your community.

"Your high-potential employees work 21% harder than their peers and bring 91% more value to the organization compared to other employees. Knowing this, it's easy to see why it benefits organizations to retain as many of their top-performing employees as possible. But how do you get them to stay? Research shows that a lack of mentoring is one of the main reasons your most talented employees decide to leave. Investing in a comprehensive mentoring program can give your high-potential employees the long-term support they want and encourage them to stay at your company— which results in better outcomes for your business. (Sophie Lee, "7 amazing Ways Mentoring can benefit your organization," Torch.io>blog, March 15, 2021).

With regard to mentoring family, "Train up a child in the way he should go, even when he is old, he will not depart from it"

(Proverbs 22:6, NKJV). In our "woke culture" today, there is mass chaos as to the definition of moral absolutes. Moral relativism has created a crisis for our children, who are confused about simply determining what is right and what is wrong. The need for us as parents to mentor our kids is paramount.

Mentor Another Person: Actions for Follow-Up, Week #19

#1: When have you mentored a coworker, a subordinate, or a child? What was the outcome? Did your mentee learn from you? Did they become your friend? When have you ignored an opportunity to be a mentor to someone at work or to your own child? What opportunity might you have missed out on?

#2: Who would be a good candidate for mentorship at your business, your workplace, and your home? Make a list. Sometimes a younger employee can even mentor their boss.

#3: What obstacles exist to your serving as a mentor? Are you worried that it would take up too much of your workday? Are you concerned that a mentee might learn your job and replace you? Are you concerned that your potential mentee might reject you when you volunteer to help them?

#4: What sacrifices will you need to make in order to be a mentor? Obviously, if you're devoting a significant amount of time to assisting a junior manager, a new assistant, or your own son or daughter, you are sacrificing hours that you could otherwise use to earn more money on the job or read a book at home. If it's your business, you may need to invest more money in your mentee. This means that when you pay higher wages to your mentee, it will pay off later in terms of increased worker productivity, worker loyalty, and possibly a succession plan for your business.

#5: If you fail to mentor a successor for your business, you may not have a means to retire in ten years. If you're a parent, with your son or daughter now an adult in ten years, will they adopt your moral, spiritual, and cultural values without your ever having taught them those beliefs?

#6: Starting today, take at least one person from the list you made on day #2 and start the mentoring process. At work, ask that employee if they would like you to mentor them.

#7: Ask the Lord to guide you in teaching the first person you decided to mentor, and request guidance as to whom else you can help. Meditate upon how you will assist the person you wish to mentor and identify whom else you might help both at work and home.

Chapter 24
Week 20
Principle: HEALTH and HEALING

Are there Biblical principles for Physical Healing?

We are addressing the question of whether the Bible provides us a foundation for physical healing.

Indeed, there are 26 specific examples of Christ healing people in the New Testament. These include healings of paralysis, leprosy, blindness, deafness, and raising the dead, among others. (A list of Jesus' Healings, www.christianhealingtoday.com). In the Old Testament, as well, there are 12 examples of God's healing, including leprosy, the plague, and the raising of the dead. Additionally, there are occasions where God did a corporate healing, including people bitten by poisonous snakes and infected by the plague. (Healing in the Old Testament (voiceofhealing.info). Also, John points out that "Jesus did many other things as well. If every one of them were written down, I suppose that even the whole world would not have room for the books that would be written." (John 21:25, NIV). Finally, when Jesus went to his hometown of Nazareth, " because of their unbelief, he couldn't do any miracles among them except to place his hands on a few sick people and heal them." (Mark 6:5, NIV) So, even in Nazareth, in spite of their unbelief, Jesus still performed healings.

There is zero evidence that Jesus ever refused to heal anyone who asked. In fact, without asking, Jesus approached the paralyzed man at the Pool of Siloam and asked the man if he wanted to be healed. (John 7-9 NIV).

In contrast, there is no biblical evidence that Jesus ever made anyone rich who asked for wealth. In Luke 12:13-14 (NIV) Jesus refuses a man's request to settle a financial inheritance dispute between him and his brother: Someone in the crowd said to him, "Teacher, tell my brother to divide the inheritance with me and Jesus replied, "Man, who appointed me a judge or an arbiter between you?" Then he said to them. "Watch out! Be on your guard against all kinds of greed: Life does not consist in an abundance of possessions."

Most importantly, Jesus healed a paralyzed man in order to show the Pharisees he is empowered to forgive sins: The Lord addressed the Pharisees, "I, the Messiah, have the authority on earth to forgive sins. But talk is cheap — anybody could say that. So, I'll prove it to you by healing this man." Then, turning to the paralyzed man, he commanded, "Pick up your stretcher and go on home, for you are healed." (Luke 5:20-24 NIV).

In Luke 9:1-2, NIV, Jesus tells his disciples to go out into the world and preach the Gospel and heal the sick. Christ doesn't limit his healing to his own ministry. Of course, we, today, as Christian believers, are Jesus's own followers.

Indeed, according to Acts, 3:1-8 (NLT), Peter, unsolicited, heals the paralyzed beggar, "Peter and John went to the Temple one afternoon to take part in the three o'clock prayer service. 2, As they approached the Temple, a man lame from birth was being carried in. Each day, he was put beside the Temple gate, the one called the Beautiful Gate, so he could beg from the people going into the Temple. 3, When he saw Peter and John about to enter, he asked them for some money.

4, Peter and John looked at him intently, and Peter said, "Look at us!" 5, The lame man looked at them eagerly, expecting some money. 6, But Peter said, "I don't have any silver or gold for you.

But I'll give you what I have. In the name of Jesus Christ, the Nazarene, [a] get up and [b] walk!"

7, Then Peter took the lame man by the right hand and helped him up. And as he did, the man's feet and ankles were instantly healed and strengthened. 8, He jumped up, stood on his feet, and began to walk! Then, walking, leaping, and praising God, he went into the Temple with them."

This is perfect evidence of Christ instruction to us today to "heal the sick," just as the apostle Peter healed the crippled man at the temple. Indeed, there is no evidence that this man ever had faith in Christ or even knew who Jesus was.

We can extrapolate from the crippled man's healing that lack of faith by the person healed is not an impediment for the healing to occur. However, the person calling for God's healing (Peter) is required to at least possess a tiny "mustard seed's" worth of faith in order to facilitate the healing.

A few years ago, I asked one of my investment clients, Roger, (not his real name), if I could pray with him for his healing. The client was suffering from cancer. The cancer was terminal and had disfigured the man's face. He wore a bandage to cover the disfigurement. Although he allowed me to pray for him, he expressed no faith that God would heal him. He was undergoing an experimental treatment for his cancer at that time. I prayed for his healing out loud as we were having lunch at a local café. I did not speak to him again for a couple of months. When I did call him, he advised me that the cancer was totally in remission and that he would schedule plastic surgery to repair the disfigurement. I exclaimed, "Praise the Lord for your healing." His response was simply that the experimental treatment had cured his cancer. There was no attribution of the healing to God and no expression of gratitude either.

On another occasion, one of my investment clients, Susan, (not her real name), related a story about her healing from lung cancer. She had been employed by a local grocery chain for over 20 years at the time. However, she was a smoker and was diagnosed with terminal, stage 4, lung cancer. The doctor did not prescribe any treatment for her. He simply sent her home to die. She was in her mid-40's at that time and became severely depressed as she awaited her death. She was not a Christian and did not even believe in God.

Yet, as the months went by, she felt stronger, her energy levels increased, and she was restless. She requested her old job back at the grocery store and was allowed to return to work. Her conversation with me took place over 20 years later, and she had never been sick again. She told me that she did not know why or how she was healed. Yet, she was also never thankful for her healing because she did not believe in the creator who made her well again.

Are some Pastors of mainline Christian denominations today afraid to preach a healing gospel? Obviously, as Jesus admitted, simply saying to a man, "Your sins are forgiven," doesn't require any supernatural power from God. However, where the rubber hits the road is when you tell the wheelchair bound woman to stand up and walk. If no one is getting healed in your church, are faith and hope really present? In John 14:12, NIV, Christ tells his disciples, "Truly, truly, I say to you, He that believes on me, the works that I do shall he do also, and greater works than these shall he do; because I go to my Father."

If we are going to do works equal to and greater than the miracles of Jesus during his earthly ministry, surely healing the sick is one of those works.

Another cop out we sometimes see in the church is Pastors and church members simply saying, "We are not gifted in the healing of the sick." However, Jesus did not specify that only certain disciples were to heal the sick. He did not say, "If you don't feel you're gifted to heal people, then the requirement to heal the sick doesn't apply to you." Jesus simply did not put an asterisk after his command to heal the sick or preach the gospel.

What is God's prerequisite for a Christian to be able to heal the sick or cast out a demon? Faith

In Matthew, 17: 15-20, NIV, Jesus chastises his disciples for lacking sufficient faith to cast out a demon from a possessed man. "When they came to the crowd, a man approached Jesus and knelt before him. 15 "Lord, have mercy on my son," he said. "He has seizures and is suffering greatly. He often falls into the fire or into the water. 16, I brought him to your disciples, but they could not heal him."

17, "You unbelieving and perverse generation," Jesus replied, "how long shall I stay with you? How long shall I put up with you? Bring the boy here to me." 18, Jesus rebuked the demon, and it came out of the boy, and he was healed at that moment.

19, Then the disciples came to Jesus in private and asked, "Why couldn't we drive it out?"

20, He replied, "Because you have so little faith. Truly I tell you, if you have faith as small as a mustard seed, you can say to this mountain, 'Move from here to there,' and it will move. Nothing will be impossible for you." (Matthew 17:14-21, NIV).

According to Jesus, tiny faith, the size of a mustard seed, is all we need to do works greater than what Christ did when he walked the earth.

However, as a result of the fraud evident in many television healing ministries, Bible-based healing pastors have often been maligned unfairly in local and national media. Peter G. Popoff was a German American television evangelist and faith healer. According to Wikipedia, "he was exposed in 1986 for using a concealed earpiece to receive radio messages from his wife, who gave him the names, addresses, and ailments of audience members during Popoff-led religious services. Popoff falsely claimed God revealed this information to him so that Popoff could pretend to cure them through faith healing. He went bankrupt the next year, but made a comeback in the late 1990s. Beginning in the mid-2000s, Popoff bought TV time to promote "Miracle Spring Water" on late-night infomercials and referred to himself as a prophet."

Again, according to Wikipedia, "In April 2021, HBO aired a documentary entitled "A Question of Miracles" that focused on faith healer and televangelist, Benny Hinn... Wikipedia explains that Hinn offered full access to his events by the HBO team. The documentary team then followed seven cases of "miracle healings" from Hinn's crusade over the next year. The film's director, Antony Thomas, told CNN's Kyra Phillips that they did not find any cases where people were actually healed by Hinn. Thomas said in a New York Times interview that "If I had seen miracles {from Hinn's ministry}, I would have been happy to trumpet it... but in retrospect, I think they do more damage to Christianity than the most committed atheist."

An elderly Christian investment client of mine, Linda (not her real name), was stricken with lung cancer. She enthusiastically embraced the teachings of Benny Hinn for her healing. This very sick lady attended one of Hinn's healing crusades in hopes of being cured. Unfortunately, she died a couple of months later.

Meanwhile, prosecutors and courts have frowned upon parents who pray for the healing of their children in lieu of obtaining conventional medical treatment for terminal illness and life-threatening health conditions.

Courts in Wisconsin and Oregon recently decided two cases involving faith healing that resulted in the death of a child. "In Wisconsin, parents who had relied on spiritual healing to treat their diabetic 11-year-old daughter were found guilty of second-degree reckless homicide. In Oregon, parents were acquitted of manslaughter charges in the death of their 15-month-old daughter, but the girl's father ultimately was convicted of a lesser charge of criminal mistreatment." (Faith Healing and the Law, Robert W. Tuttle, 8/31/2009, /www.pewresearch.org/religion/2009/08/31/faith-healing-and-the-law/). In neither case did the parents pursue timely conventional medical treatment with physicians.

However, speaking for myself and most evangelical Christians, I will certainly pursue divine healing as well as conventional medical treatment in the event I or a family member is facing life-threatening illness. This is where the theological distinction between my belief in the ability and desire of God to heal me and the fact that, despite prayer, most people with terminal cancer and heart disease do not get healed. First, only a percentage of people with fatal illnesses pray for healing. Secondly, as we have shown, everyone who asked Jesus for healing during his earthly ministry was cured. More importantly, "he was pierced for our transgressions, he was crushed for our iniquities; the punishment that brought us peace was on him, and by his stripes we are healed." (Isaiah 53: 5-7). Christ's sacrifice at the cross allowed for both the forgiveness of all our sins and the physical healing of our bodies.

Finally, according to the Lord's prayer, we ask God that "your kingdom come, your will be done in earth as it is in heaven." (Matthew 6:9-13). We know that there is no sickness in heaven. Consequently, God/s will on earth is that there should be no sickness here on earth either.

However, many faithful Christians pray for healing every day and pass away, often in pain and without healing. This is a dilemma for Christians who cannot reconcile the biblical healings of Jesus with the death of their loved one whom they prayed for. Consequently, many Christians simply conclude that healing only occurred during Jesus's ministry on earth and during the ministry of the apostles. They question, however, is it the will of God for everyone seeking healing to be healed or only a select few to be healed?

Yet, what is the will of God? According to the Bible, with respect to salvation, "I urge, then, first of all, that petitions, prayers, intercession, and thanksgiving be made for all people—for kings and all those in authority—that we may live peaceful and quiet lives in all godliness and holiness. This is good and pleases God our Savior, who wants all people to be saved and to come to a knowledge of the truth." (1 Timothy 2:1-4 NIV).

The will of God clearly then is that all people "be saved." However, we know that billions of human beings are not even professing to be Christians and are dying in their sins without salvation every day. They may be Hindus, Buddhists, Muslims, atheists, agnostics, or some other religion. So, God's will is certainly not being done in terms of the salvation of the human race.

Consequently, when Christ urges his disciples to "Go and heal the sick," he is fully aware that not every human being will be healed. Although his will is that all the sick be healed, Christ knows that the "wages of sin is death." (Romans 6:23 KJV). We know that the will of God is for all people to be healed for two reasons. First, every person who asked God for healing during his earthly ministry was healed. Second, Jesus did not tell his disciples, "Go and heal the sick – except for the Romans, the pagans, and the Samaritans." He made no exception for his order to heal people. However, bear in mind that people were still getting sick and dying while Jesus was healing other people during his ministry. Jesus said to his disciples, "Go into all the world and preach the gospel to every creature. He who believes and is baptized will be saved; but he who does not believe will be condemned. And these signs will follow those who believe: In My name… they will lay hands on the sick, and they will recover." (Mark: 16:15-18).

Both God's will for all to be saved and all to be healed is frustrated every day. So, why is God's will in both cases never accomplished for all people?

The answer again is rooted in the sin of man. In Matthew 5:48, Jesus says, "Be perfect, therefore, as your heavenly Father is perfect." Jesus is saying that the will of the Father is that we would be without sin. Obviously, none of us is without sin. Again, the will of God is thwarted by our imperfection, our sins collectively.

The bottom line here is that until sin is eradicated in this world, many people will die without salvation, and many people will not be healed. However, this does not negate the will of God that we would all accept Christ and all be healed.

Now, what is the practical application of God's will for our healing? First, the Bible does not prohibit Christians from seeking a physician's help to get well when they are sick or injured. In fact, according to Jesus," It is not the healthy who need a doctor, but the sick." Although Christ was referring to sin and not physical sickness, he made his point in terms of physical illness and the need for medical assistance. There are no Bible passages that otherwise discourage Christians from going to a doctor. Secondly, of course, there are many cases of healing in the Old and New Testaments by prayer. According to James, 5:14-16, NIV, "Is anyone among you sick? Let them call the elders of the church to pray for them and anoint them with oil in the name of the Lord. And the prayer offered in faith will make the sick person well." There is certainly no admonition here against also seeking the assistance of a physician. However, there is a statement that "the prayer offered in faith will make the sick person well." Again, we know that not every person who has been prayed for by the elders of the church has been made well. Yet, we believe that faith on the part of the elders is imperative for healing to occur. Finally, we know that many people do receive God's healing after receiving prayer.

What do we say then to the sick person, prayed for in faith, who is still sick long after the elder's prayer? Worse yet, what do we say to his wife when he dies shortly after the elders, in faith, prayed for him?

The only proper response is that due to the sins of the human race, God's will for that woman's husband to be healed has been frustrated on earth. As difficult as that is for the family to hear, it is true. Due to our sin, we cannot expect to gain eternity with Christ in this life. Due to sin's corruption, our bodies will eventually fail. This may be due to cancer, a heart attack, a car wreck, or some other disease or accident. The will of God for our freedom from sickness, death, and sin will be accomplished permanently in heaven. It is important to know that the prayed for person's death is not due to that person's sin, but the sin of all people. In John 9:1-3, NIV, the disciples question Jesus, "As he went along, he saw a man blind from birth. 2, His disciples asked him, "Rabbi, who sinned, this man or his parents, that he was born blind?" 3, "Neither this man nor his parents sinned," said Jesus, "but this happened so that the works of God might be displayed in him."

Even though Lazarus was brought back from death to life by Jesus, he, himself, too, eventually died like every other human being. We can hope for healing for ourselves and our loved ones in this life based upon the healings of Jesus and the words of Paul exhorting the sick to seek the prayer of the church elders. Yet, we must remember that even these prayers are subject to the will of God for that person's longevity on earth. In Jeremiah, 1:5, NIV, God says, "Before I formed you in the womb, I knew you, and before you were born, I consecrated you." In the New Testament, Jesus says, "Why even the hairs on your head are all numbered." Luke 12:7 NIV.

It stands to reason that a God who "formed you, "knew you in the womb," and "numbered the hairs on your head," would certainly know how long you will live.

Based upon the authority of holy scripture, we can conclude that healing is still available today. It is the perfect will of God that all people be healed. However, for healing to be universal, God's perfect will that sin be eradicated must also be fulfilled. Until man stops sinning and death is destroyed, healing will be sporadic and sometimes incomplete. Yet, "the effectual fervent prayer of the righteous man availeth much." James 5:14-16 KJV. As scripture instructs, we should be praying for and healing the sick every day. However, we must bear in mind that we will only see the healing when it is consistent with the will of God in a fallen world.

The Prayer for Healing the Sick

Most traditional Christian denominations also teach that God can still heal people today. Catholics and Greek Orthodox churches also teach the healing method described in James 5:14-16, NIV, and referenced earlier. "Is anyone among you sick? Let them call the elders of the church to pray over them and anoint them with oil in the name of the Lord."

However, many pastors take it a step further.

When Jesus healed a person during his ministry, he often spoke directly to the sick person. In John, 5:8-9, NIV, Jesus heals a

155

paralyzed man who had been sitting by the healing pool for 38 years waiting to be cured by the waters. "Then Jesus said to him, "Get up! Pick up your mat and walk." 9, At once, the man was cured; he picked up his mat and walked." Importantly, the bible passage does not indicate that this man possessed faith in Christ or knew about his ministry.

Years later in the ministry of Peter and John, Peter finds a crippled beggar sitting by the city gate begging for money. "Now a man who was lame from birth was being carried to the temple gate called Beautiful, where he was put every day to beg from those going into the temple courts. 3, When he saw Peter and John about to enter, he asked them for money. 4 Peter looked straight at him, as did John. Then Peter said, "Look at us!" 5, So the man gave them his attention, expecting to get something from them.

6, Then Peter said, "Silver or gold I do not have, but what I do have I give you. In the name of Jesus Christ of Nazareth, walk." The man was instantly healed. (Acts, 3:2-7, NIV).

It is significant that in this passage, there is no evidence that the paralyzed man had faith in God or even knew who Jesus was.

When Jesus cast demonic spirits out of a man, he spoke directly to the demon(s). and they pleaded with him. "When Jesus stepped ashore, he was met by a demon-possessed man from the town. For a long time, this man had not worn clothes or lived in a house but had lived in the tombs. 28, When he saw Jesus, he cried out and fell at his feet, shouting at the top of his voice, "What do you want with me, Jesus, Son of the Most High God? I beg you, don't torture me!" 29, For Jesus had commanded the impure spirit to come out of the man. Many times, it had seized him, and though he was chained hand and foot and kept under guard, he had broken his chains and had been driven by the demon into solitary places.

30, Jesus asked him, "What is your name?"

"Legion," he replied, because many demons had gone into him. 31, And they begged Jesus repeatedly not to order them to go into the Abyss.

32, A large herd of pigs was feeding there on the hillside. The demons begged Jesus to let them go into the pigs, and he gave them permission. 33, When the demons came out of the man, they went into the pigs, and the herd rushed down the steep bank into the lake and was drowned." (Luke, 8:26-37, NIV).

Based upon Jesus and Peter's speaking directly to the sick person and the demon, many evangelists conclude that we also should speak directly to the sick person and command in the name of Jesus that he be healed. Given the Biblical examples of Jesus and Peter, the Word of Faith approach here is consistent with Holy scripture.

When "good people" die, and "bad people" get healed.

We wonder why our family member or close friend died of cancer, while someone we know who hated God and never prayed was cured of cancer or heart disease.

Sometimes I have heard it justified by someone saying, "Well, God cured the bad person to give him an opportunity to see God's goodness, repent, and be saved. God took the good person because he was needed in heaven."

Yet, we really have no idea why the "Good person" died, and the "bad person" lived.

Similarly, we are shocked when we learn that convicted murderers confess Christ and are saved by the grace of God. Chris Watts strangled his pregnant wife and two young daughters to death in 2018. He was convicted and sentenced to life in prison. Later, he accepted Christ and now claims to be born again. Likewise, serial killers Jeffrey Dahmer and "Son of Sam," David Berkowitz, professed an encounter with Christ and salvation by his grace. In the cases of these men, they were already serving a life sentence without the possibility of parole. Consequently, they could not have been incentivized to claim their redemption in order to curry favor with a naïve parole board to let them loose. (A&E, True Crime Blog: Stories and News, Laura Dorwart, 6/28/2021, Chris Watts, David Berkowitz and Other Infamous Killers Who Found God in Prison - A&E True Crime (aetv.com)).

Obviously, we can't be certain whether the confessions of these men who committed horrific murders and sins against God can be trusted. Only Christ knows if their newfound faith is real or fraudulent. However, the Bible gives witness to a similar conversion. Paul, although not the murderer himself, approved of the stoning of the martyr, Stephen, by the crowd who killed him. Moses had murdered an Egyptian prior to God's calling him to lead his people out of bondage to the Pharaoh. Finally, Jesus, himself, forgave the thief on the cross of his sins and promised to take him to paradise.

Yet, in January 2022, famed Christian rapper, Phanatic, after 30 years of Christian music, writing, and Christian education, renounced all belief in Christ. Phanatic had been a co-founder of the famed Christian rap group, "The Cross Movement," and a two-time Grammy nominee. Phanatic simply renounced Christianity in a 24-minute Facebook video. He claimed that he had "harbored doubts" for a number of years. Phanatic had studied the Bible extensively. With a master's degree from Westminster Theological Seminary, he had taught apologetics, preached the word, and led Bible studies. (Christian Headlines, Prominent Christian Rapper, Phanatic, publicly renounces Christianity, Milton Quantanilla, 1/21/2022, https://www.christianheadlines.com/contributors/milton-quintanilla/prominent-christian-rapper-phanat).

Jesus, speaking to his disciples, said, "You did not choose me, but I chose you and appointed you to go and bear fruit—fruit that will last." (John 15:16, NIV) We scratch our heads, trying to understand how serial killers may be chosen for the kingdom of God, and 30-year adherents to the gospel reject salvation.

Like healing, salvation too, is impossible to understand without knowing the sovereign will of God. We should not be wasting our time asking why one is chosen by God for salvation or healing, and one is not. Our job is to pray in faith for both.

Prayers for Healing – Actions for follow-up.

#1: When have you ever prayed for the healing of a friend or loved one? What was the result? Did they recover from their illness or injury? If they did not recover, were you angry with God? If you were mad at God, repent of that sin now and ask God to guide you in all future prayer for healing.

#2: Did you ever pray for your own healing? Regardless of whether you prayed for a recovery from the flu, a broken arm, or cancer, what was the result? If your illness was cured or you recovered from an injury, did you thank God, or did you attribute your healing to the doctor or the medicine you were given? If you haven't thanked God yet, thank him now. In Luke, 17:11-14, NIV, Jesus heals the lepers, "11, Now on his way to Jerusalem, Jesus traveled along the border between Samaria and Galilee. 12, As he was going into a village, ten men who had leprosy [a] met him. 13, They stood at a distance and called out in a loud voice, "Jesus, Master, have pity on us!"14 When he saw them, he said, "Go, show yourselves to the priests." And as they went, they were cleansed.15 One of them, when he saw he was healed, came back, praising God in a loud voice. 16 He threw himself at Jesus' feet and thanked him—and he was a Samaritan. 7, Jesus asked, "Were not all ten cleansed? Where are the other nine? 18, Has no one returned to give praise to God except this foreigner?" 19, Then he said to him, "Rise and go; your faith has made you well."

Jesus made a point of singling out the 9, lepers who never returned to thank him for curing them of the horrific disease of leprosy. So, should we also always remember to thank him for healing?

#3: What obstacles will prevent you from praying for the healing of yourself or others? You might respond that you lack sufficient faith in God to pray for friends or family to be healed. However, in Matthew, 9:24-29, a father asks Jesus to help him with unbelief in his request that Jesus drive a demon out of his son, "I do believe; help me overcome my unbelief! When Jesus saw that a crowd was running to the scene, he rebuked the impure spirit. "You deaf and mute spirit," he said, "I command you, come out of him and never enter him again." So, ask God for the faith you need, and he will grant it.

#4 What sacrifices will you need to make in order to pray for others' healing? If you are angry at God for any reason, you must make a sacrifice of repentance for that anger prior to petitioning God for the healing of yourself or others. You may be holding a grudge against God because someone close to you died or because you feel God abandoned you in a time of need. Let go of that resentment before asking the Lord for healing.

#5 If you don't pray for a friend or family member who is sick now, will you regret it in the future if that person dies or their illness worsens? What is the cost of your prayer other than the time it will take you to pray?

#6 Start praying today for that person who is physically sick, injured, or mentally ill. If you don't have a friend or relative needing that prayer, check with co-workers or friends of your friends. Surely, you know someone who needs healing prayer.

#7 Give God thanks and glory for hearing your prayer and coming to your aid or the aid of a loved one.

Chapter 25
Week #21
Principle: FREEDOM

Freedom vs. Tyranny

Communism and socialism oppose freedom in America and globally today. Can you achieve true prosperity if you cannot go to church or worship God? Can you achieve true prosperity if you cannot start a business, make a profit, or earn a paycheck based on your merit as a hard worker? Can you achieve true prosperity if you are muzzled when you oppose your government, advocate for a political idea, or are denied the right to vote for your leaders? These are the hallmarks of tyranny. Unless you are free, you will never be prosperous.

We, individually, cannot achieve true prosperity if we are denied the freedoms upon which America was founded as a Judeo-Christian nation. Specifically, each of us should pursue religious, political, economic, and intellectual freedom. This means petitioning our government, our schools, and our corporations for redress whenever these freedoms are denied to ourselves or our brothers and sisters across America. Utilizing the 21 principles to achieve personal success and having a great family is not enough. If we and others are dictated to or propagandized by our government, our schools, or our corporations, we can never call ourselves prosperous people.

Religious Freedom

The first Christian Pilgrims arrived in what is present-day Massachusetts from England aboard the Mayflower ship in 1620. They were seeking freedom from the persecution of the Church of England. After the American Revolution, the founders of America enshrined the doctrine of religious freedom in the U.S. Constitution under the 1st amendment. Two types of religious freedom were established in the Constitution.

First, the establishment clause prohibits our government from creating a state religion that all Americans would be required to adhere to. Secondly, the 1st amendment, under the free exercise clause, allows all Americans to freely exercise their religious beliefs. Consequently, regardless of whether you are a Christian, Buddhist, Muslim, Hindu, or atheist, you are free to worship or not worship God in whatever manner you wish. Recently, a high school football coach was fired in Bremerton, Washington, because he knelt down and prayed on the field after every football game. In the case of Kennedy vs. Bremerton School District, 6/27/2022, the school district argued that the coach's prayers had a coercive effect upon high school students watching their coach pray, and the students might feel obligated to join him. However, the U.S. Supreme Court found that the district had violated the coach's freedom to exercise his religious beliefs as guaranteed by the 1st amendment. The coach's lawyer, Paul Clement, represented the coach for free, on a pro bono basis. This was because he believed in the cause of freedom for religious speech. Otherwise, the coach could not have afforded the cost of an attorney to fight a school district that could easily hire high-priced legal counsel. The case dragged on for over 8 years, and the coach persevered in his efforts for vindication and to recover his job. As a result, the Supreme Court sent a message to every school district and local government across America that their employees may exercise their right to pray and practice their religion. If this coach and his attorney had not persevered, today, cities, counties, and public schools might still be intimidating their employees with threats of firing if they exercised their freedom of religion.

In another Supreme Court case, Carson vs Makin, 6/21/2022, the Court held that if the state of Maine provides funds to parents for private school tuition, they must not discriminate against or prohibit religious or Christian schools from receiving those tuition payments. Maine state law only allowed public tuition payments for non-sectarian private schools. Christian and all religious schools were barred from receiving state funding. The Court ruled that if Maine made public funding available for secular private Education, it must also provide it to Christian and other religious schools. Consequently, the State of Maine was in violation of the Constitution's mandate to allow all Americans the free exercise of their religion. Again, pro bono attorneys from the Christian advocacy group, Alliance defending Freedom, represented two families that the State of Maine had prohibited from receiving public tuition assistance to attend Christian schools. If the attorneys had not provided their legal representation for free, those families would probably not have had the financial means to send their children to Christian schools. Again, as a result of the perseverance of the families and their lawyers in this litigation, no state may discriminate against Christian and religious schools with public funds. If this case had not been litigated, any state would have been able to exclude Christian schools from public funding.

We need to raise up phalanxes of Christian attorneys who will challenge the woke anti-Christian policies of the American left in order to restore and then preserve religious freedom in the United States.

Consequently, Christians are still facing an uphill fight to assert their 1st amendment rights in the public marketplace. In the future, Christian businesspeople may be reluctant to take a Bible based stand against discriminatory laws for fear of fines, lawsuits, and public reprobation that can force them out of business.

Political Freedom

Freedom from Racism

You may be adhering to the 21 biblical principles outlined in this book and suffer discrimination because of your skin color today. Although great strides in civil rights have been made since Martin Luther King made the "I have a dream speech" in 1963, even today, there is still some discrimination against African Americans and other minorities in America. Deadly race-based confrontations with local police in African American neighborhoods were exemplified by the George Floyd case. Examples of police brutality against African Americans are not numerous and do not reflect the attitudes of most law enforcement officers. However, when they occur, they are egregious, racially divisive, and corrupt our culture further.

On top of this discrimination, corporate America has also unleashed a torrent of discrimination against Caucasians based on Critical Race Theory.

In February 2021, a whistleblower at Coca-Cola claimed that the company forced employees to take a seminar teaching them to "be less white." The whistleblower posted photos of a seminar giving tips to "be less white," including "be less arrogant, be less certain, be less defensive, be humbler, listen, believe, break with apathy," and "break with white solidarity." The materials claimed that white people in the United States and other western nations are "socialized to feel that they are inherently superior because they are white." ("Major Corporations had Woke Training Exposed in 2021," Tyler O'neill, 12/24/2021, Fox Business.com).

Critical Race Theory is divisive and teaches that systematic racism against black people and other minorities is embedded in American culture. As a result, white people, whether they recognize it or not, are oppressing African Americans and other minorities with their "white" culture. Critical Race Theory is intended to create white guilt and make minorities feel hopeless and beaten down. Finally, as a result, animosity between whites, blacks, and other minorities is encouraged and maximized. This theory is the antithesis of the teachings of Christ. While teaching white people to be less "arrogant" and "humbler" is good, all people need to learn those lessons.

Major corporations recently were caught *propagandizing* their employees with the critical race theory curriculum, including American Express, Bank of America, Lowe's, and Pfizer, among others.

The teaching of Critical Race Theory has spread from the corporate boardroom to the elementary and high school classrooms.

"In Cupertino, California, an elementary school required third graders to rank themselves according to the "power and privilege" associated with their ethnicities. Schools in Buffalo, New York taught students that "all white people" perpetuate "systemic racism" and had kindergarteners watch a video of dead black children, warning them about "racist police and state-sanctioned violence." And in Arizona, the state's education department sent out an "equity toolkit" to schools that claimed infants as young as 3 months old can start to show signs of racism and "remain strongly biased in favor of whiteness" by age 5. The nation's largest teachers' union outright endorsed the teaching of CRT to public school students in an agenda item it passed. The National Education Association vowed to "share and publicize" information "already available on Critical Race Theory — what it is and what it is not" and fight back against legislation that would ban CRT from school curricula." ("Yes, Critical Race Theory is being Taught in Public Schools," Washington Examiner, 7/12/2021).

We cannot enjoy true prosperity when we are encouraged by the government and corporate America to engage in a race war with our brothers and sisters whose skin is a different color. As parents, we need to attend school board meetings and protest this indoctrination of our children. As corporate employees, we should be speaking out against woke managers who would attempt to brainwash us into hating others based upon so-called "white privilege." Personally, of my six children, two are my African American sons, and four of my kids are Caucasian. None of my kids are privileged based on the color of their skin.

Many conservative teachers are leaving the profession in frustration over the leftist curriculum promoted by the National Education Association. My youngest son, Elliott, is African American. He is now a high school sophomore. Last year, in 8th grade, he received the award for being the student displaying the most Christian character in his class. He did not suffer discrimination in his Christian school and certainly was not the victim of any "white privilege." Critical Race Theory is being employed as a wedge to create racial turmoil, which could result in violence and rioting. The decades of progress and success against racism achieved by the civil rights movement are disregarded and of no value according to Critical Race Theory. Martin Luther King achieved victory over white racism, which was particularly virulent in the South in the 1960s. King emphasized that all people should be judged by the content of their character, not the color of their skin. Yet, critical race theory denies this progress and finds racism systemic in every school, government, corporation, and white person's head. Consequently, we must reject the Critical Race Theory and the race hatred which it inspires. Finally, we need to embrace the successes of America's civil rights movement and press on to eliminate all forms of racial discrimination.

Political Freedom from Government using Corporations and Social Media to Suppress Free Speech.

"I wholly disapprove of what you say and will defend to the death your right to say it."

—Voltaire

Our constitution guarantees us the freedom of expression: "Congress shall make no law respecting an establishment of religion or prohibiting the free exercise thereof; or abridging the freedom of speech, or of the press; or the right of the people peaceably to assemble, and to petition the Government for a redress of grievances." (U.S. Constitution, 1st Amendment)

How can I be truly prosperous if my government directly or indirectly muzzles the expression of my opinion and purposely prevents me from listening to the views of anyone who opposes its policies and opinions?

In the last few years, we have witnessed the suppression of the views of physicians who oppose the Government's coronavirus policies based on different data compilations or theories of disease etiology. We have seen social media banish politicians who offer conservative viewpoints on political issues. Parents of school children have been repeatedly investigated by the F.B.I. for speaking out on education issues at local school board meetings across America, as a former F.B.I. Special Agent, I am ashamed of a premier law enforcement agency that would spy on parents attending their children's school board meetings.

Yet the constitution did not address social media. Of course, social media did not exist in 1791 when the 1st amendment was ratified. Today, TikTok, Twitter, Facebook, Google, and other social media have often been accused of employing tactics to suppress conservative viewpoints, commentary, speeches, and essays. In many respects, social media has supplanted the government as the arbitrator of what people should think and the filter of public expression of opinion.

Economic Freedom

Real Prosperity means defending economic freedom in America.

If our government creates too many financial and legal obstacles to starting a business, buying a franchise, or investing in the stock market, it will become virtually impossible for us to achieve real financial prosperity. If the U.S. government continues to bury the American people in debt, in order to pay it back, the taxes on our income and our children's income will be oppressive.

Barriers to economic freedom

As of February 1st, 2022, the U.S. Government has racked up over $30 trillion in debt. (U.S. National Debt Surpasses $30 Trillion: What this means for you," E. Napoletano, 2/16/2022, Forbes. Com) The millennial generation, Gen Z, and succeeding generations will be responsible for paying it back. This will require higher taxes and less money for Americans to start businesses, save money, and invest for a nice retirement. Politicians have lured the American people into electing them based upon promises of "free money," free education, and free or subsidized health care. The non-partisan Tax Policy Center estimates that 57% of all American households paid no federal income taxes in 2021. However, many received Covid relief funds, tax credits, and stimulus checks. ("57% of U.S. Households paid no Federal Income Tax Last year as Covid took a Toll, Study says," Robert Frank, 3/25/22, CNBC.com).

Real prosperity means that we don't incur debts that we can never afford to repay. Secondly, we don't take on enormous debt and saddle our sons, daughters, and grandchildren with the duty to

169

repay it. Finally, as responsible citizens and families, we repay our financial obligations. According to the Bible, "The wicked borrow and do not repay, but the righteous give generously." When we owe over $30 trillion, it will be extremely burdensome to repay that debt with higher taxes. How can we ever afford to "give generously" under the weight of that debt?

We should vote and petition our elected leaders to start balancing the federal budget and repaying this mountain of debt.

Saving and Investing

Giving back to God

Before you start saving, make a commitment to give a portion of your income each month to the Lord through your local church. If you don't have a church, there are many Christian charities in need of funds worldwide. If you are not a Christian, select a charity to be the beneficiary of your generosity.

Real financial prosperity is the product of frugality, monthly savings, and investing in risk assets.

Frugality

Establish a personal budget or a couple's budget if you are married. Simply, list your total net income each month on the left side of a sheet of paper. On the right side, list your monthly debts, i.e.. Rent or mortgage, utilities, medical bills, etc. Include in your debts at least 10% of your net income for savings and investment. Allow at least 5% of your net income for recreation, i.e., going to dinner, skiing, or vacation savings.

Monthly Savings

Take the 10% savings and put it in the bank. Accumulate at least a (4) month net pay emergency fund before you start investing. The establishment of your emergency fund may require (6) to (12) months of saving diligently. However, in the event of a job loss or sickness, this will prove invaluable as your safety net.

Investing

After building a (4) month emergency savings stockpile, begin investing at least 10% of your monthly income in stock and bond mutual funds for your retirement as directed by your financial advisor. Investment in the stock market through mutual funds or individual stocks is referred to as investment in risk assets. Many people fear the stock market as a result of warnings from parents and grandparents about various stock market crashes. However, in order to build a successful strategy for retirement, exposure to stock market investments is necessary. This is true because stocks and investment real estate provide the highest long-term return on capital. You should speak to a financial advisor about how to use tax-deferred plans such as your 401k, 403b, IRA, and Roth IRA plans. These investment vehicles will allow you to defer taxes, compound your interest, and thereby maximize the number of dollars working for you. Also, a financial advisor can address what percentage of your investments should be allocated to stocks, bonds, and money market accounts.

With a $30 trillion debt, the expectation is that regardless of whether Democrats or Republicans control the White House, tax rates will increase in the future as the government attempts to pay its debt. The risk of our government someday defaulting on its debt will compel Congress to raise taxes. A government default on its treasury debt would spell financial disaster for all Americans. If the U.S. government cannot pay its bills, the value of the U.S. dollar would plummet, inflation would skyrocket, the stock market would crash, and massive poverty would ensue.

Your best personal defense against this scenario is to construct a diversified investment portfolio and minimize personal debt. You should buy and pay for your home as soon as possible. In addition, if possible, add investment in real estate. Real estate might be a rental home that is cash flow positive or at least cash flow neutral. This means that the rental income will at least defray the cost of owning the investment real estate. All of your investments should be coordinated with your financial counselor.

Social Security

Absolutely, do not depend upon Social Security for your main source of retirement income if possible. Your personal savings and investment must be your number one source of retirement income unless you are blessed with a guaranteed pension from government or corporate funds. The Social Security Administration's own website concludes that Social Security benefits are now expected to be payable in full only until 2037, when the trust fund reserves are projected to become exhausted. ("The Future Financial Status of the Social Security Program, Stephen C. Goss, Social Security Bulletin, Vol. 70, No. 3, 2010, Social Security. Gov). In other words, by 2037, Social Security is out of money, and you probably won't get paid.

Courage to Speak out against Government Policies, Corporate rules, and Woke Culture.

You cannot achieve and enjoy true prosperity if American culture erodes and dies. True prosperity requires critical thinking. As my favorite bumper sticker reads, "Don't believe everything you think." I would add to that: "Don't believe everything the woke media tells you." Therefore, take courage and persevere in your efforts to protest and reject every attempt by the government to promote tyranny in our culture.

Chapter 26
CONCLUSIONS

Follow the steps for all twenty-one principles on a daily basis. At the end of twenty-one weeks, check your status with each of the twenty-one principles. List the ones with which you have had the most success on one page. For those principles with which you enjoyed the greatest success, give yourself an A or B depending upon your confidence level in mastering them. These may be areas of your life in which you were already strong. For instance, if you have been a patient person most of your life, you probably found that week #12 was very easy for you, so you should earn an A or B for patience.

On the other hand, if you struggle with courage, then this is one of the habits you should list in the minus column on the opposite page. Grade yourself honestly. If you're doing poorly on courage, give yourself a D or an F for that category. All principles for which you are showing Ds and Fs should be prioritized for scheduling for additional weeks. You should then take at least two additional weeks to redo those principles. For instance, if you gave yourself a D in courage, schedule two weeks to focus on that principle, simply repeating days #1 through 7 each week. At the end of that two-week period, grade yourself again. If you still cannot justify giving yourself at least a B in courage, block out the next two weeks to repeat the process again until you are confident that your courage level has improved to at least a B. Getting to the B level should mean that you feel you are mastering that principle, and as time goes on, your level of courage will continue to accelerate.

Once you reach a level of confidence with any of these principles, the growth you see in that character trait should be exponential. When you reach the point that you are confident with your progress in one of these principles, it will be time to consult with your friends, family, and business associates. Ask friends, family, and coworkers if they see a change in you in that area of your character. If they do not, then you will know that this is an area that requires still more focus for additional two-week sessions. Most of the time, those friends and family will be telling you about the positive changes they see in you before you even ask them! They, like you, will be simply amazed at the change in you as a result of your focus on improving your character.

Changing your character is ultimately a consequence of repeatedly practicing these principles daily until they become habitual. Remember, there is zero reason for failure. Simply persevere in focusing on the change you want until it happens. When you start seeing these changes in your personality, character, and behavior, you will be excited about your future and wonder why you didn't do this earlier. This process should be taught in every high school and college.

In our present culture, where moral depravity is exalted in our media, you will stand out as a unique leader. However, many segments of our society will resent your moral clarity, especially when it inevitably leads to your success. Western culture, including media, universities, and most churches, no longer believe in, appreciate, or even tolerate moral absolutes. Even the concept of God is muddled. New age beliefs in a multiplicity of gods, the idea that we are all gods, or the total absence of God is becoming more prevalent. The new environmentalism touting a Mother Earth God is also popular. Eastern ideas regarding Buddhism, Hinduism, and reincarnation are heartily promoted. Biblical truths such as the Ten Commandments are viewed as archaic, as is the Bible itself. The attendance and membership of young people in traditional Christian churches have also plummeted. Consequently, when you achieve business success by practicing the twenty-one virtues outlined in this book, expect criticism. If you achieve your success as Hugh Hefner did by displaying erotic pictures of naked girls in a magazine, you are virtually untouchable by the mainstream media. However, success resulting from adherence to biblical principles will open your life up to scrutiny. Obviously, since we all fall short of the standard of perfection, there are skeletons in each of our closets. Expect the secular culture to search out your imperfections and broadcast them aloud. This, again, is a business risk for those who embrace biblical truth.

The Risk of Self-Righteousness and Arrogance: A Note of Caution as You Make Progress

As your self-image develops and grows as a consequence of your ethical habits, be alert for a tendency to exalt yourself above others. Remember, pride comes before the fall. Not only will you be subject to more scrutiny as others view your new lifestyle and behavior, but you may be tempted to treat coworkers, subordinates, and even family members with a tone of condescension or contempt. You should periodically review week # 11's principle, humility. As your successes pile up, so will your sense of self-importance and a tendency to think of yourself as better than others.

When I was hired as a stockbroker years ago, I was assigned to be an understudy to a man who was the number-one revenue producer in our office. This man had achieved awards for outstanding sales results year after year. He was also in a leadership role in a large Christian church in our community. He was a very outgoing and confident individual. However, after a few weeks, I learned that he had been suspended. Subsequently, it was revealed that he had been forced to resign due to his taking advantage of his clients through his unethical conduct.

We are all vulnerable to temptation. That vulnerability is often greatest when we are riding the crest of the wave of success.

Potential Roadblocks to Completing This Program Successfully

Do not expect instant change in all twenty-one categories. Some principles will be more difficult to master, and several will be easier. God has granted you the ability to master all twenty-one principles in his word. Yet you will never obtain perfection. Even the apostle Paul, after many years as a Christian evangelist, said, "I do not understand what I do. For what I want to do I do not do, but what I hate I do." (Romans 7:15, NIV).

On New Year's Eve, the one-hundred-pound overweight man joins the health club, resolving to work out every day, lose weight, and get into shape. He starts working out each day for the first two weeks. By March, however, he's working out one day every other week, he hasn't lost weight, and he's about to give up trying to get his body in shape. Starting out with enthusiasm and the best of intentions is simply not enough. Expectations in the short run must be realistic if he is to achieve the long-term goal. He would be better served by establishing first a short-term goal of working out one day per week for the first two months. At each two-month interval, he should then increase his workouts by one day each week. Short-term success will incentivize long-term efforts to reach the long-term objective of losing a hundred pounds and getting in shape.

Like any problem, the best solution is usually the result of breaking the issue down into its component parts. Those parts, in our case, will be short-term goals. If you're struggling to establish courage, don't begin with challenging yourself to march into your boss's office and issue him or her an ultimatum to either grant you a promotion or you'll quit. You might first want to summon the courage to gently request that promotion if courage is a problem for you.

Similarly, when implementing each principle each week, make a written journal notation of each success. For example, if the principle is kindness, make a written note of the date and what actions you took. Do not record your failures. Give yourself a high five for each success. At the end of each week, find a way to reward yourself for the victories you achieved.

A second red flag for all of us is stress. If you're experiencing a difficult day, or you are overwhelmed by your boss, or your son is rebelling at home, cut yourself some slack and take a few days off from this program. Devotion to embracing these principles should never be just another burden on your shoulders. If completing the week's reading and assignment becomes just another stress in your life, you will eventually surrender and abandon the program.

Motivation

If you are working on developing self-discipline this week, remember that bad habits provide a certain amount of pleasure. If you're trying to lose weight and you find yourself downing a pint of Häagen-Dazs chocolate ice cream, what's the problem? It tastes fantastic! You'll wait until tomorrow and then fast for two days!

Bad habits can also provide security. You want to master the principle of courage, yet you are battling the desire for security, safety, and not being disliked. You want to challenge the extra charges you see on the bill from your child's daycare provider, but you're afraid to confront the manager. It's always safer to keep your mouth shut, blend in, and move on. These are obstacles to motivation. Your drive to master the principle must be greater than whatever positive reinforcement the bad habit is providing you with.

Only by first recognizing that roadblock to your motivation can you defeat your past and establish a new habit.

The only true obstacle to following the road map to success outlined in this book is your willingness to focus your time, energy, and will upon each of the twenty-one principles. I encourage you to carry this book with you every day. Reread the principle for the week you are in each morning before work or school. Review the step for the day each morning and resolve to put it into practice that day. In the evening, take fifteen minutes before bedtime to review your successes or failures with that principle for that day. Determine where you will improve tomorrow and congratulate yourself for your diligence each evening. If you are a believer, thank God as well for his help.

You are fully equipped by your creator for success. Jesus said, "I have said these things to you, that in me you may have peace. In the world you will have tribulation. But take heart; I have overcome the world." (John 16:33, ESV).

Success is contingent upon two factors: your commitment and your perseverance.

Commitment

Are you willing to be absolutely committed to mastery of these twenty-one principles? Let me give you my personal best example of commitment. When I was a twenty-three-year-old law student in San Francisco, my apartment was less than a block away from a local ice cream shop. I love hot fudge sundaes. Soon I was the shop's best ice cream customer. I would stop by after classes, carrying my law books, and get my hot fudge sundae fix every day. Within a few months, I had gained over twenty pounds. I made a commitment to diet, boycott the ice cream shop, and start exercising.

I recalled back to my freshman year of college when I joined the Notre Dame boxing team. To my knowledge, only Notre Dame, the military academies, and a handful of other colleges continue to offer boxing as a collegiate sport. Boxing at Notre Dame culminates with an intraschool boxing tournament called the Bengal Bouts each March.

My coach instructed me that, to be successful as a boxer, I needed to run at least two miles per day. For at least four months, I ran two to three miles each day and worked out at the gym to get myself in shape to fight. By the time I reached the tournament in March, I had lost fifteen pounds, and I was in excellent physical shape. After the Bengal Bouts and getting knocked around in the tournament, I never returned to boxing. However, hearkening back to my time as a boxer, I decided to commit to losing twenty pounds of ice cream sundaes by adopting an exercise regimen.

So, I began persevering in working out every day for the rest of my life. At first, I ran just one mile per day. I ran the streets of San Francisco, jogging along Geary Street west toward the ocean every morning from my Richmond District apartment. At first, working out was difficult because I was overweight and sedentary, and there was a traffic light stopping me at each block. As I developed my endurance over the next two months, I stretched my runs to one and a half miles and finally to over two miles per day. Now, for more than forty years, I have maintained this healthy addiction. Perhaps one day every couple of months, I will miss a run due to early and late meetings at the office, a cross-country flight, or a medical appointment. Even when I do miss a day, I'm obsessed with guilt until the next day when I run again. This is my positive addiction.

I have been able to create the same type of positive addiction with writing. I made a commitment to write no less than one chapter per day, seven days a week. Similar to committing to running two-plus miles every day, I find that I miss a day writing every month or two. Again, I feel guilty on the day I miss, and I'm determined the very next day to prioritize my writing again.

These positive addictions are keys to success, just as negative addictions are keys to failure. Alcohol, drugs, food, and sex addictions will absolutely ruin your life. With negative addictions, when you're "on the wagon" and not feeding your addiction, anxiety increases until you take another drink, snort another line, or eat another dish of ice cream.

Likewise, with positive addictions, anxiety will increase if you're not feeding the addiction. So, make sure you allocate time for your positive addictions before you adopt them. Like negative addictions, they will be difficult to let go of once created.

These twenty-one principles require a lifetime commitment. Once committed, you will revolutionize your mindset, your behavior, and your lifestyle as your opportunities for success skyrocket.

Perseverance

Finally, after initiating your commitment to these principles, your perseverance with these habits will inoculate you against failure. Weekly perseverance at each new principle will result in that positive addiction, which will be self-reinforcing for you.

Perseverance, of course, is crucial not only for adherence to these principles but for success in your spiritual, family, and work life.

Final Thoughts

I wrote this book in part to address the moral crisis in America. Without moral clarity and direction, we are aiming at nothing and hitting that target every time. The 21 principles enunciated here are guideposts on a clear path to true success and prosperity. The political, religious, and economic freedoms I describe are the foundation upon which those principles can be developed in your life. Failure to lay that foundation of freedom for all Americans will radically undercut your ability to exercise those 21 principles for success and prosperity in your own life.

Your first priority in achieving real prosperity should be the development of the 21 principles of character as habits in your life as an individual. Once you have established your self-discipline in that regimen, you should start focusing on your opportunities to exercise your liberty as an American. This can be accomplished by attending your local school board meeting, educating yourself on political issues, and voting responsibly to protect our freedoms. Longer term, more Americans should be adopting and fostering children. My wife, Cindy, and I, of course, have adopted five kids. We were able to raise our kids with biblical values, enroll them in Christian schools, and take them to church. You may not be called to adopt kids as we were. However, I am certain that you, too, are called to a ministry. It may be in a local church, volunteering in a charity, or becoming active in a friend's local political campaign. There is a myriad of ways to confront evil in our culture today.

Never apologize for the Bible, biblical principles, or your Christian beliefs. As Jesus said, "Whoever is ashamed of me and my words, the Son of Man will be ashamed of them when he comes in his glory and in the glory of the Father and of the holy angels." You will stand out as a leader in your family and your workplace when you choose courage in the face of temptation to be silent when your beliefs and principles are challenged.

In the event you do not have a personal relationship with our Lord and Savior, Jesus Christ, today is the day for you to come to Salvation. Simply repeat the following prayer.

"Hello, Jesus, let me introduce myself. I am _____. I declare that I am a sinner. I need a savior; I invite you into my life and my heart today. I accept you as my Lord and Savior. I thank you for shedding your blood and dying on the cross for my sins. From this day forward, I pledge to follow you."

After you have prayed this prayer, find a solid Bible based local Church and start attending on Sundays.

May the Lord bless you in achieving real prosperity!